FINAL BATTLE

The Next Election Could Be the Last

DAVID HOROWITZ

Humanix Books

www.humanixbooks.com

Humanix Books

FINAL BATTLE by David Horowitz
Copyright © 2022 by Humanix Books
All rights reserved

Humanix Books, P.O. Box 20989, West Palm Beach, FL 33416, USA
www.humanixbooks.com | info@humanixbooks.com

Library of Congress Cataloging-in-Publication Data is available upon request.

Humanix Books is a division of Humanix Publishing, LLC. Its trademark, consisting of the words "Humanix Books," is registered in the Patent and Trademark Office and in other countries.

ISBN: 978-163006-224-8 (Hardcover)
ISBN: 978-163006-222-5 (E- book)

Printed in the United States of America
10 9 8 7 6 5 4 3 2 1

To all my countrymen and women, dead and alive, who dedicated their lives to making America the free country for all races, ethnicities and creeds that it is, and that the left is determined to destroy.

Contents

Prelude vii

1. Elections Matter 1

2. Insurrection and Impeachment............................ 17

3. Inauguration.. 45

4. Open Borders 61

5. Reimagining the Law.. 91

6. Corona Control.. 115

7. Reimagining the World.................................... 139

8. Orwellian Acts 155

9. The Fall of Afghanistan 171

10. The November Rejection.................................... 191

11. Where Are We Headed? 205

Acknowledgments.. 213

Endnotes... 215

Index.. 251

Prelude

For the 1,357 inhabitants of Butler, Pennsylvania, the high point of 2020 was, without question, the October 31 campaign rally for President Donald J. Trump. Three days before the election, on a chilly Pennsylvania night, more than 50,000 people gathered in the airport of this tiny Steel Belt town, located 35 miles north of Pittsburgh. It was Trump's fourth rally of the day, and the crowd had come to hear the candidate's blunt delivery, unpredictable asides, and familiar jibes at Biden and the Democrats. They came to chant "USA! USA!" and to hear once more his promise to make America prosperous, safe, and great again.[1]

Trump's final seventeen hours of campaigning had included more than 3,000 miles of flights and motorcades, 367 minutes of rallies, and—in the words of one *Wall Street*

Journal reporter, "five awkward and hilarious stage dances to [the popular song] 'YMCA.'"[2] A Trump rally was always an entertainment.

At one point in the evening, the crowd became so ardent—as similar rallies had before—that it began to chant "We love you!" and did so over and over, until Trump responded: "Thank you. Don't say that. I'll start to cry and that wouldn't be good for my image."[3] It was an uncharacteristically emotional moment, displaying a self-awareness and even self-deprecation, that went generally unacknowledged by Trump's legion of haters.

In the 21 days between his recovery from the Covid he had contracted at a White House gathering, and the November election, the tireless candidate had held a total of 45 rallies, each attended by thousands and even tens of thousands of supporters. When Election Day arrived, Trump returned to the White House in the presidential helicopter. *Marine One* touched down on the South Lawn at 3 a.m.

When Trump arrived home, he was so exhausted that he overslept and was 45 minutes late for a 7:00 a.m. interview on *Fox and Friends*. After the show, Trump did a radio interview with a conservative talk show host in Pennsylvania. "The ultimate poll," he told the interviewer, "are these massive crowds that are showing up to rallies. Nobody's seen anything like it ever."[4]

At 11:08 p.m. a current of optimism rippled through the White House where members of the Trump team had gathered to watch the returns. When the key state of Florida went to Trump, and by a larger margin than in 2016, it seemed to signal the tipping of enough battleground contests to carry him to victory. He had been told by his pollster John McLaughlin that he needed 66 million votes to win; he was on track to get 74 million. But 21 minutes later, Fox declared the Republican state of Arizona for Biden with only 30 percent of the votes counted, and the air came out of the Trump team balloon.

Trump called his friend, Fox chief Rupert Murdoch to try to get him to withdraw the Fox election report. But to no avail. For the next hours Trump had a hard time accepting that the tide had turned and he was going to lose. For a straw to grasp onto, he could look to Pennsylvania, where he was still ahead by 690,000 votes. But unknown to him a massive influx of late votes was going to strip him of that lead, and in other battleground states as well. As media outlet after media outlet declared the election for Biden on the basis of incomplete returns, Trump attempted to fight back.

"They're trying to steal the election," he said in a televised address to his supporters on November 4. "And we can't let that happen. . . . Frankly, we did win this election."[5] But the forces seeking to seal the win for Biden proved overwhelming. They even included prominent Republicans who were concerned about the consequences of a disputed result, and declared the election over to avoid that prospect. Facing impossible odds, Trump closeted himself in the White House, where he remained silent for the next few days.

On Saturday, November 7, Trump left the White House for the first time that week to golf at his club in Sterling, Virginia. As he was about to tee off at the seventh hole, he received a call from his son-in-law Jared Kushner who told him the networks were about to call the election in Pennsylvania for Biden. Pennsylvania's twenty electoral votes would give Biden the 270 he needed to win the presidency. According to eye-witnesses, "Trump took the call calmly. He nonchalantly strolled through the grass as he talked with his son-in-law for a few minutes, handed the phone back to an aide, and then finished the last twelve holes of the course as a motorcade of two dozen golf carts—filled with Secret Service agents, law enforcement, and White House aides—trailed behind him."[6]

While Trump was still finishing his golf game, club members had gathered to shout their encouragement, telling him he had won, and to finish the fight. "Don't worry, Trump said. "It's not over yet."

1

Elections Matter

IN A CONSTITUTIONAL democracy, elections are sacred rites. They register the will of the people as sovereign, and make ballot boxes the ultimate courts of appeal.

In creating the American Republic, its founders' greatest fear was the threat posed by partisan factions. They called the threat a "tyranny of the majority," and feared that a victorious party would gain authority in all aspects of public life, and use the powers of the federal government to impose a one-party state on everyone else. A tyranny of the majority could destroy democracy from within.[1] To prevent America's descent into such a tyranny, the Founders crafted constitutional rules that were designed to force compromise, and blunt the destructive passions that partisan agendas unleashed.

The Founders' fears inspired a system of "checks and balances," which took the form of separations and divisions of powers, and their decentralization. These measures were designed to frustrate the ambitions of the majority, and limit the governmental powers it might control. The skepticism and caution of the Founders reflected their Christian faith, which recognized that human beings are flawed by nature, and their ambitions are not to be trusted.

Among the provisions the Constitution made to thwart unruly schemes were these: indirect elections through a state-based Electoral College, an independent judiciary able to veto the wishes of legislative majorities, and a federal system that put both law enforcement agencies and voting regulations in the hands of state legislatures rather than the central power in Washington, D.C.

The constitutional system the Founders devised, endowed citizens with unprecedented freedoms, framed as limits to governmental powers. Their purpose was to protect the people from governmental abuse, and to encourage them to challenge orthodoxy in all its forms.

They had a paradoxical result as well. At the same time the constitutional order decentralized power, it also acted as a unifying force. By protecting electoral minorities, it enabled the community of diverse, "voluntary associations" to prosper and grow, and to come together as one people to meet the challenges posed by enemies abroad and at home.

So long as the principles and procedures written into the Constitution remained universally binding, the republic was destined to endure. In the nation's 250-year history, only a conflict as irreconcilable as the one pitting freedom against slavery had torn its fabric so irreparably as to precipitate a civil war. All other conflicts were resolved by compromise and self-restraint. If an election was lost, there was always an opportunity, provided to the defeated, to regroup and win the next one.

America now faces a crisis that many compare to the onset of the Civil War. One prominent characteristic of the fractures in the current body politic, is that all the moderating institutions described above, which were designed by the Founders to soften the edges of political conflict and unify the nation, are under siege by the Democrat Party and its supporters. These include the Electoral College and Senate, which Democrats seek to abolish as "*un*democratic"; the independent judiciary, which Democrats want to make an appendage of the legislative branch by packing the Supreme Court; the federal system which reserves to the states, rights and powers not specifically assigned to the bureaucracies in Washington; and the integrity of the electoral system, which Democrats refuse to protect by validating ballots through voter IDs.

Most dangerous of all, by insisting that the electorate be divided by race; by demonizing their opponents as white supremacists and racists, and by attempting to criminalize religious beliefs, Democrats have conducted a sustained assault on the spirit of compromise that binds the union together, and set the nation on the path to a one-party state.

The Divisions That Confront Us

The divisions between domestic factions, coupled with the attacks on moderating institutions, now threaten to destroy the traditions that bring Americans together. They undermine the possibility of bipartisan solutions to common problems like viral pandemics and civil disorders. Americans speak now in different and antagonistic political languages, and the two parties are so polarized that the electoral process itself is under attack.

Concerns about the integrity of the electoral process are not new, but had already reached a critical point during the 2000 presidential election because of a disputed ballot count in Florida. Ultimately, the Supreme Court had to be brought in to adjudicate the dispute, which it resolved in favor of the Republican candidate, George W. Bush, making him America's 43rd president. This electoral result was never accepted by the defeated Democrats, who referred to Bush as "selected" rather than "elected," and therefore illegitimate.

In 2003, this fracture in the body politic led directly to an unprecedented reversal of Democrats' support for the war in Iraq. It was a war that George W. Bush had initiated and Democrats had authorized. A Democrat presidential primary happened to be taking place in the spring of 2003, at the same time as the American invasion. When an anti-war activist named Howard Dean looked to be running away with the nomination, Democrats *en masse* turned against the war they had authorized. Nothing had changed on the battlefield to ignite this opposition. Democrats justified their defection by demonizing the president whom they already considered a political imposter because of the contested Florida vote. Democrats claimed Bush that had lied about the intelligence regarding "weapons of mass destruction" in order to deceive them into supporting the war. This was a transparently false charge, since Democrats sitting on the Intelligence committees had access to the same information that Bush had relied on. But this fact didn't prevent Democrats from running their 2004 presidential campaign on the theme *Bush lied, people died!*—a slander that drove a wedge between the parties that would have grave consequences for both the war and the political future.[2]

The Carter-Baker Commission Attempts to Fix the Problem

To address the problem that had so weakened American unity and the nation's ability to defend itself, former Democrat president Jimmy Carter joined forces with former Republican Secretary of State James Baker. Together they created the Carter-Baker "Commission on Federal Election Reform." After a year-long investigation, they issued a report with a series of recommendations designed to strengthen the integrity of the election process and re-unify the nation.

Among their key conclusions were recommendations to increase voter ID requirements; to minimize the use of mail-in ballots, which "remain the largest source of potential voter fraud"; to ban ballot harvesting by third parties; to purge voter rolls of all ineligible or fraudulent names; and to allow election observers to monitor the ballot counting without restraint or obstruction.[3]

By 2019, a year before the Biden-Trump election contest, the country had become so politically polarized that Democrats launched a massive campaign to change the election laws. They chose to do so in ways that would reverse every one of the Carter-Baker recommendations, and make election fraud easier. They justified these efforts as attempts to end race-based "voter suppression," as though blacks and other minorities were incapable of complying with the same rules that whites did.

To implement their changes, the Democrats filed nearly 300 lawsuits, many focused on the battleground states. The suits were designed to expand the use of mail-in ballots, dilute voter ID requirements, permit third-party ballot-harvesting, and make legal other practices that Carter-Baker had specifically sought to eliminate.[4] Democrats followed these initial attacks on election integrity by dispatching 600 lawyers and 10,000 volunteers to as many states as possible, three months before the 2020 presidential election—including all the battleground states. Their goal was to change the election laws by loosening and overturning regulations that had been instituted to make the process more secure.[5]

Trump Fights Back

Alarmed by the Democrats' attack on election procedures, Trump responded with a warning on his Twitter feed: "With Universal Mail-In Voting (not Absentee

Voting, which is good), 2020 will be the most INACCU-RATE & FRAUDULENT Election in history. It will be a great embarrassment to the USA." Then he threw out the question: "Delay the Election until people can properly, securely and safely vote???"[6]

It was a characteristic mis-step. Trump didn't have the authority to delay the election, but the implication that he might try anyway, fed the Democrats' ongoing suspicions that Trump would use his executive powers to stop the election and remain permanently in office. Months earlier his opponent Joe Biden had made exactly that charge: "Mark my words," Biden said in April. "I think he is going to try to kick back the election some-how, come up with some rationale why it can't be held."[7] As with the accusations that Bush had lied, Democrats' extravagantly low opinions of Trump encouraged their supporters to take such speculations seriously.

To Trump and his supporters, the meaning of the new rules was clear. The Democrats were going to try to steal the election. According to polls, 61 percent of Democrats regarded Trump and his supporters as "racists" and 54 percent regarded them as "ignorant"—signs of how far factional polarization had gone.[8] Their hyper-ventilating hatred of Trump and his voters was so great that they were ready to consider all means available to stop him. On the other hand, there was little that Trump could do to prevent the damaging effect the new rules would have on his chances. He was forced to watch, for exam-ple, as Democrats in Pennsylvania—a key battleground state with 20 electoral votes—changed the election rules to favor themselves, even though they were violating the U.S. Constitution in doing so.

Article II, Section 1, Clause 2 of the U.S. Constitution clearly stipulates that the rules governing elections are the jurisdiction of the legislatures of the states. This provision was designed to decentralize and democratize the voting process, thwarting the efforts of a power grab by one party through institutions whose officials were un-elected. Disregarding this clear constitutional order, the Democrat legal Squads by-passed the Pennsylvania legislature, which was controlled by Republicans, and appealed directly to the state Supreme Court on which Democrats had a 5-2 majority.[9]

The Democrat-dominated State Supreme Court responded by illegally authorizing a series of new election rules dramatically favoring the Democrats. For example, as bestselling author Mark Levin explained: "Just months before the [2020] general election, that court rewrote the state election laws to eliminate signature requirements or signature matching, eliminate postal markings that were intended to ensure votes were timely, and exten[d] the counting of mail-in ballots to Friday at 5:00 p.m." (state law had set a hard date and time, Election Day, which was the previous Tuesday at 8:00 p.m. E.T.). In other words, the Democrats had fundamentally altered Pennsylvania's election laws and nullified the federal constitutional role of the Republican legislature.[10]

The loosening of the rules, and the obstruction of Republican poll-watchers, made "ballot dumps" easier and led to dramatic spikes in the results. A Pennsylvania

Senate hearing three weeks after the election, was presented with sworn testimony that in one such dump, Biden received roughly 570,000 votes—or 99.4 percent of those cast, while Trump received only 3,200 or 0.6 percent ballots submitted.[11] Biden's margin in winning Pennsylvania was about 81,000 votes.[12]

In an attempt to close the barn door before it was too late, Trump's team and supporters filed 61 lawsuits, almost none of which were ever heard by the judges, who rejected them out of court.[13] They did so ostensibly on procedural grounds but more likely out of partisan prejudice or fear of the damaging consequences to their institutions if they overturned a presidential election result.[14] Also dismissed by these same courts were thousands of affidavits and declarations, testimony given by witnesses in a variety of state venues, election analyses published by think tanks and legal centers, and video as well as photographic evidence of possible corruption in the ballot-counting process.[15]

The Most Votes Ever Cast

When the votes were counted and the results were in, two factors stood out as particularly painful for Trump. The first and most important was the conviction that he had won. For more than four years Democrats and their media allies had waged a relentless slander campaign against him, calling him "worse than Hitler," a "white supremacist," a "sexist," a "racist," a "traitor," and even a "mass murderer."

The latter accusation was made by Trump's presidential opponent Joe Biden on the very eve of the election. Before the 70 million television viewers of the final presidential debate, Biden accused Trump of killing every Covid-19 patient who had died since the pandemic first took root:

> 220,000 Americans dead. If you hear nothing else I say tonight, hear this: Anyone who's responsible for not taking control—in fact, not saying, I take no responsibility, initially—anyone who is responsible for that many deaths should not remain as President of the United States of America.[16]

Despite the constant drumbeat of these lies, when the 2020 election results were in, Trump had outperformed every incumbent president before him. Every one, including Barack Obama, had received fewer votes in his run for a second term. But in 2020, Trump miraculously increased his margin by 11.2 million votes, making his total of more than 74 million, the most votes ever cast for an American president in the past.

On the other hand, to believe that Biden had won, one would have to believe that a mentally challenged candidate, who campaigned from his basement, who could hardly sustain a train of thought and couldn't get through a campaign speech without a teleprompter, whose crowds were generally in the low double-digits, while Trump was drawing thirty and fifty thousand supporters to his

rallies—one would have to believe that this fumbling figure received nearly 12 million more votes than Barack
Obama at his peak.[17]

Trump was also confident he had won because despite
all the irregularities and unconstitutional practices by
the Biden campaign, Biden's margin of victory was still
razor thin. Roughly 159 million total votes had been cast
in the 2020 presidential election. Biden's margin of victory was 43,000—or 0.027 percent of the total. If the votes
illegally cast in Pennsylvania and two other battleground
states had been properly thrown out by the courts, Trump
would have won.[18]

A Second Painful Fact

Trump's recognition of this gut-wrenching fact was accompanied by another—the knowledge that in five of the
six battleground states, Republican majorities ruled the
legislatures but had refused to enforce the constitutional
provision that would have declared the Democrat rules
unconstitutional, and secured his victory. Despite his direct appeals to these Republican legislators, they had sat
on their hands and refused to either investigate or rectify
the illegal proceedings.

As the new year approached, Trump was running out
of authorities he could appeal to if he was going to reverse the election result. The Trump team had filed 61
suits in the lower courts nearly all of whom refused to
examine the evidence. The only hope they had left was

a lawsuit filed by the state of Texas. The Texas suit was backed by 126 of 196 Republicans in the House and 19 Republican states that filed motions in support.[19] Trump referred to the case as "the big one." It sought to delay the vote by presidential electors in the battleground states of Georgia, Michigan, Pennsylvania, and Wisconsin, arguing that voting procedures in those states had been changed in violation of their own state laws, and of the Constitution. These illegal votes in turn devalued the votes in other states like Texas by weighting the overall election result.

On December 11, despite its conservative majority, the Supreme Court refused to hear the suit. "The Supreme Court really let us down," Trump tweeted in disappointment. "No Wisdom, No Courage!"[20] There would be no justice for him from the judiciary.

To Disagree Is an Act of Treason

In a typical comment by the political left, Biden spokesman Mike Gwin said, "The Supreme Court has decisively and speedily rejected the latest of Donald Trump and his allies' attacks on the democratic process." Gwin added: "This is no surprise—dozens of judges, election officials from both parties, and Trump's own Attorney General have dismissed his baseless attempts to deny that he lost the election. President-elect Biden's clear and commanding victory will be ratified by the Electoral College on Monday, and he will be sworn in on January 20."[21]

The betrayals of the Republican legislatures were accompanied by the betrayals of other prominent Republicans who owed Trump and American voters more fealty than they were able to muster. This included Attorney General William Barr, Vice President Mike Pence, and Senate Majority Leader Mitch McConnell, all of whom could have stepped forward to support his quest for a fair hearing but didn't.

Throughout Trump's efforts to rectify a corrupt election, Democrats deliberately and consistently confused the act of questioning an election result with an attack on democracy itself, which they pointedly associated with treason.[22] "I think this borders on treason," House Majority Leader Steny H. Hoyer told the *Washington Post*. "He is undermining the very essence of democracy, which is: You go to the poll, you vote and the people decide. There's no doubt that the people decided."[23] Echoing the general tenor of the media response, the *Post*'s star Washington reporter, Dana Milbank, wrote: "President Trump broke any number of laws and norms during his ruinous four-year reign. He just added one more on the way out: treason."[24]

Democrats and their partisan media leveled this grave charge calculating that to do so would intimidate their opponents into inaction. To be accused of being an enemy of democracy and a traitor to your country is obviously a damaging accusation for anyone with political ambitions, particularly with a media that functions as an echo-chamber for such charges. This was no doubt a significant factor in the defections of Republican elected officials.

Despite the Democrats' claim that challenging a vote is treason, the fact remains that such challenges happen all the time and are perfectly legitimate within a democratic framework. Dictatorships outlaw critics of their elections; democracies don't. But raising hypocrisy to whole new levels, the Democrats themselves had questioned the results of all three Republican presidential election victories since 2000, agitated to decertify electors, and attempted to reverse the results.

"Stop the Steal"

In a last-ditch effort, Trump announced that he would hold a "Stop the Steal" rally on January 6, 2021, the date the House of Representatives was scheduled to convene to certify the electors and confirm the election result. Because he was aware that lawlessness had become an accepted norm in Democrat cities since the death of George Floyd in May 2020, and since there were bad actors battling each other from both sides during those riots, Trump offered to provide 10,000 federal National Guard troops to protect the Capitol on January 6. His offer was rejected by the Democrat Mayor and Black Lives Matter supporter, Muriel Bowser.[25] Trump's offer was also rejected by Nancy Pelosi and the Capitol Police.[26]

Trump's "Stop the Steal" rally took place at the Ellipse, a park located about 2 miles from the Capitol. The president spoke for well over an hour to an estimated 100,000 supporters. His speech focused on the "weak" Republicans who failed to protect the integrity of the election. A second theme was the necessity of building a new Republican Party that was ready to fight to put America first and restore its traditions. He summoned the crowd to achieve this by primarying the weak Republicans in the 2022 midterms and replacing them with Republicans that "fight like hell." A long third section of his speech was devoted to describing the "evidence" of fraud that Democrats were denying existed.

"For years, Democrats have gotten away with election fraud," Trump told the crowd. "Weak Republicans," he said were responsible for that fact. "I think I'm going to use the term, the weak Republicans. You've got a lot of them. . . . They've turned a blind eye, even as Democrats enacted policies that chipped away our jobs, weakened our military, threw open our borders and put America last. . . . This year, using the pretext of the China virus and the scam of mail-in ballots, Democrats attempted the most brazen and outrageous election theft and there's never been anything like this. So pure a theft in American history. Everybody knows it."

"You have to get your people to fight," he continued. "And if they don't fight, we have to primary the hell out of the ones that don't fight. You primary them. . . . Because you'll never take back our country with weakness. You have to show strength and you have to be strong. We have come to demand that Congress do the right thing and only count the electors who have been lawfully slated, lawfully slated. I know that everyone here will soon be marching over to the Capitol building to peacefully and patriotically make your voices heard."

The bulk of the speech was devoted to laying out the evidence his supporters had amassed of election fraud that Democrats were alleging didn't exist—the dead voters, the illegal voters, the people who no longer lived in the state but voted, the districts in which more votes were turned in than there were voters in the district; the bad practices—mail-in ballots, unsecured drop boxes, third-party ballot harvesting that had been illegally introduced into the electoral process to make cheating easier.

"In Pennsylvania," Trump said, "the Democrat secretary of state and the Democrat state Supreme Court justices illegally abolished the signature verification requirements just 11 days prior to the election. So think of what they did. No longer is there signature verification. . . . Eleven days before the election they say we don't want it. You know why they don't want it? Because they want to cheat. That's the only reason. Who would even think of that? We don't want to verify a signature?"

It was a good question, but to raise it, according to the Democrats, was treason.

Trump's speech ended with these words: "We're going to try and give [the weak Republicans] the kind of pride and boldness that they need to take back our country. So let's walk down Pennsylvania Avenue."[27]

2

Insurrection and Impeachment

WELL BEFORE TRUMP finished his speech, several thousand members of the crowd of 100,000 broke off from the rally at the Ellipse and began the long trek to the Capitol. Most of them remained outside the building, but somewhere in the neighborhood of 600 to 800 managed to enter. They were led by a handful who broke in through the front door and adjacent windows. A melee ensued that pitted an understaffed and under-equipped Capitol Police force against a small segment of the crowd composed of radical right-wing groups who had come to fight. There was no concerted defense of the Capitol perimeter, so most of the demonstrators walked in unimpeded and unopposed.

Over the months that followed, more than 650 of the occupiers were formally charged with crimes ranging from trespassing to resisting arrest and conspiracy to organize the event.[1] According to the U.S. Attorney's Office for the District of Columbia, at least "165 defendants were charged with assaulting, resisting, or impeding officers or employees."[2] There were, in addition, two separate thefts of House Speaker Nancy Pelosi's laptop computer and lectern.[3] Of all those arrested, ninety-nine were connected to radical right-wing groups like Oath Keepers and the Proud Boys.[4] Most of those apprehended were ordinary citizens, as were the 100,000 who gathered to hear Trump's "Stop the Steal" speech and didn't break into the Capitol. Unlike the youths who had torn up and looted American cities all summer, the overwhelming majority came to peacefully protest.[5] Their crime was trespassing.

According to National Public Radio, approximately forty-four of the defendants, 7 percent of the protesters apprehended, were actually charged with conspiracy to coordinate their actions with others to commit the break-in and protest.[6] An FBI investigation later corroborated this, concluding that there was little evidence the whole protest was coordinated.[7] A Reuters report about the FBI probe said: "FBI investigators did find that cells of protesters, including followers of the far-right Oath Keepers and Proud Boys groups, had aimed to break into the Capitol. But they found no evidence that the groups had serious plans about what to do if they made it inside."[8] Added Reuters: "[T]he FBI has so far found no evidence that [President Trump] or people directly around him were involved in organizing the violence."[9]

According to the same NPR report, at least twenty-one of the defendants were Oath Keepers. Their very presence at the event should have raised red flags for the Capitol authorities.[10] Long before January 6, the Oath Keepers had been officially described by the military and law enforcement as "America's largest militia," the "most prominent anti-government group in the United States," and "the preeminent right-wing domestic extremist insider threat to the entire U.S. military."[11] Yet the Oath Keepers' leader, Stewart Rhodes, the man regarded as the originator of the break-in plan, was not arrested, investigated, or charged with any crime. In the eyes of skeptics, the only plausible explanation for this omission was "a deliberate decision by the Justice Department to protect him."[12]

In a development that fed conspiracy theories on the right, NPR investigators reported that at least 13 percent of those charged had possible ties to the military or to law enforcement.[13] In addition, there were numerous reports concerning as many as twenty "unindicted co-conspirators" named in the indictment who were not charged, leading to widespread speculation that they were FBI informants and provocateurs.[14] While the anti-Trump media dismissed such speculations as conspiracy theories, the FBI was forced to confirm that, of the eighteen men involved in a previous plot to kidnap Michigan Governor Gretchen Whitmer, no fewer than twelve were paid FBI informants. This led critics to wonder whether the FBI had foiled the plot, or encouraged it.[15]

It also raised troubling questions about the rejection of Trump's offer of 10,000 troops to guard the Capitol and the unexplained and uninvestigated failure of the Capitol Police to provide sufficient security after they had been warned that trouble was afoot. These facts led many to conclude that the whole event was a setup by Democrat Party officials and their allies in law enforcement to create an incident that would both damage Trump and justify repressive actions against his supporters.[16]

The same critics pointed to the fact that the leaders of several of the militia groups, including Enrique Tarrio, the head of the Proud Boys, were already known to be cooperating with the FBI. The demonstration itself seemed to be the brainchild of the Oath Keepers, the most prominent of these groups, whose members had been engaging in physical conflicts with Antifa and Black Lives Matter rioters during the summer violence. Later reports revealed that three of the arrested Oath Keepers were cooperating with the police.[17] According to their testimony, Stewart Rhodes had been planning a demonstration to disrupt the proceedings inside the Capitol as far back as November 2020.[18] The Capitol Police were aware of the Oath Keepers' plans because they had been alerted to them on Parler, the social media platform that gained prominence when Twitter banned President Trump from its platform.

On January 6, Rhodes typed into Signal App (a privacy-protected messaging platform) his own explanation of the protest taking place inside the Capitol: "All I see Trump doing is complaining. I see no intent by him to do anything. So the patriots are taking it into their own hands. They've had enough."[19]

Democrats on the Attack

If the right-wing militia leader saw the breach of the Capitol as a protest against Trump's inaction, the Democrats' view was its polar opposite. Speaker Pelosi set their narrative the following day: "Good afternoon. I don't know if the word 'good' is a way to describe it, because yesterday the President of the United States incited an armed insurrection against America, the gleeful desecration of the U.S. Capitol, which is the temple of our American democracy, and the violence targeting Congress, are horrors that will forever stay in our nation's history, instigated by the President of the United States. . . . In calling for this seditious act, the President has committed an unspeakable assault on our nation and our people."[20]

Pelosi's fevered attempt to describe what happened in the most lurid terms set the tone for the reactions of all Democrats, and even of many Republicans who feared attacks by Democrats for being soft on what was now portrayed as a heinous crime. Having described Trump's role in the event as treasonous, Pelosi proceeded to call for his removal from office: "I join the Senate Democratic Leader in calling on the Vice President to remove this President by immediately invoking the Twenty-Fifth Amendment. If the Vice President or cabinet do not, the Congress may be prepared to move forward with impeachment. That is the overwhelming sentiment of my caucus. And the American people, by the way."[21]

Nothing in Pelosi's narrative held up to factual inspection. Not a sentence in Trump's "Stop the Steal" speech was an incitement to violence or insurrection. The actions he urged were a show of support to strengthen the resolve of "weak Republicans" so they would oppose the certification of electors, which he claimed were fraudulently confirmed. And, if that failed, to "primary them" in the 2022 midterms. These were perfectly legitimate political tactics, which Democrats themselves had employed many times in the past.

The "armed insurrection" Pelosi accused Trump of inciting was also a fantasy, and a malicious one. Not a single firearm of any kind was confiscated from those arrested inside the Capitol—although CNN claimed, without evidence, that there was an unused pistol.[22] Nothing Trump said during the entire election campaign was an incitement to anything outside the democratic process. Moreover, if it had been Trump's intent to stage an insurrection, why would he have offered to provide 10,000 armed National Guard troops to protect the Capitol on January 6?

Initial reports of five deaths during the protest enabled Democrats to insinuate that the raucous elements in the crowd had used deadly violence, and used it against the Capitol Police. But as the facts slowly emerged, these accusations also proved to be false. Inconveniently for the Democrats and the anti-Trump media, all the deaths on January 6 were of Trump supporters, three of them from stress-related natural causes—a stroke, a heart attack, and an indeterminate "medical emergency."[23] The death of a single Capitol Police officer, Brian Sicknick, was widely misreported—by the New York Times and by

President Biden himself—to smear the protesters. It was said Sicknick's death was the result of an attack by a protester wielding a fire extinguisher who hit him in the head. In fact, Sicknick was an ardent supporter of President Trump, and he died on January 7 after suffering two strokes. The allegation that he had been struck by a fire extinguisher also proved to be false, although Democrats continued to repeat the claim long after the event.[24]

The only person actually killed in the Capitol was an unarmed 35-year-old woman named Ashli Babbitt, a fourteen-year Air Force veteran, who was shot in the head at point-blank range by a Capitol Police officer while she was threatening no one. The murder was caught on video by a reporter who was subsequently arrested for being present. His video footage was confiscated. The identity of the trigger-happy officer was concealed by Pelosi and he was exonerated after a Justice Department investigation whose proceedings were hidden from the public.[25] Democrats failed to release more than 14,000 hours of video surveillance footage of the events captured on numerous security cameras, suggesting to many that the unedited tapes contained exculpatory evidence and undermined Democrats' claims about an "armed insurrection."[26]

There was also no "desecration" of the Capitol, as Pelosi claimed, unless she was referring to her stolen laptop and lectern, which were later returned. Windows were broken, and doors were damaged along with some artifacts. But no fires were set, no historical memorabilia or statues vandalized (a common practice of Black Lives Matter radicals during their riots); no members of Congress were injured.

On the other hand, the hysteria—real and contrived—was so great that Democrat congresswoman and "Squad" leader, Alexandria Ocasio-Cortez, was emboldened to claim she was the subject of a near-death attack. "I had a pretty traumatizing event happen to me," Ocasio-Cortez wrote on Instagram. "And I don't even know if I can disclose the full details of that event due to security concerns. But I can tell you that I had a very close encounter where I thought I was going to die."[27] On examination, her story fell apart when it was revealed that the person she encountered in her office was a Capitol Police officer, not an alleged rioter.[28]

Democrats Switch Strategies

As they were hammered by critics pointing out that the facts didn't support their hair-raising narrative, the Democrats were forced to modify its adjectives and nouns to avoid ridicule. But they did so while attempting to preserve the apocalyptic threat that served their interests in accusing Trump and his followers of treason. Over time, the "armed insurrection" became known simply as an "insurrection," but—courtesy of Cori Bush (D-Missouri), head of the Black Lives Matter caucus in the House—also a "white supremacist coup attempt."[29] Announcing the formation of a committee to investigate the event, Pelosi, without evidence or logic, described its "root causes" as "white supremacy," "anti-Semitism," and "Islamophobia."[30] Senate Majority leader Charles Schumer (D-New York) compared the protest to Pearl Harbor. Other

Democrat leaders invoked such atrocities as the 9/11 attacks and even the Holocaust as comparisons.[31]

In what was perhaps the most brazen act of hypocrisy in the annals of the House, Representative Adam Schiff (D-California) actually broke down in tears during a speech on the floor in a transparently ridiculous plea to Republicans for political tolerance. "If we're no longer committed to a peaceful transfer of power after our elections if our side doesn't win, then God help us," said Schiff, who had spent the previous four years claiming—without evidence—that the 2016 election was the result of Trump's treasonous collusion with the Russians and that Trump was not a legitimate president.[32]

To sustain the fiction that January 6 was "one of the darkest days in American history," and to ramp up the furor surrounding it, Pelosi ordered a fully armed National Guard contingent of 25,000 troops to the Capitol at a cost of half a billion dollars and the erection of a razor-wire fence to surround the building.[33] She did so without protest from Mark Milley, the chairman of the Joint Chiefs of Staff, who had rejected a request from President Trump for troops when the White House was under siege from a Black Lives Matter mob that had already torched one of its gate houses.

Though she reduced the number of troops as the months passed and no one showed up to challenge them, Pelosi kept more than 1,500 troops at the Capitol for more than four-and-a half months even though no insurrectionists showed up, while she provided no evidence that an actual threat existed to justify such extreme and unprecedented measures.[34] With the collaboration of the incoming Biden administration, Pelosi then launched a search for "domestic terrorists" in the ranks of the Capitol Police.[35]

With White House backing, this spread to the Department of Homeland Security[36] and all the military services.[37] Yet an FBI probe eventually concluded that there was scant evidence of any type of organized plot to overturn the government and that, as one senior law enforcement official put it: "Ninety to ninety-five percent of these are one-off cases."[38] Even left-leaning National Public Radio's investigative reporters conceded that "a large majority of those charged have no known connections to established extremist groups."[39] Yet no apologies or second thoughts were ever forthcoming from Pelosi, or the White House or Department of Justice, or the military establishment. As a result, the idea that patriotic Trump supporters presented a "domestic terrorist" threat remained a reality for these same government agencies, and anyone for whom the White House had any credibility at all.

Among those present in the Capitol on January 6 with "no . . . connections to . . . extremist groups," was a 49-year-old grandmother who was captured six months later in the still operating dragnet of the Department of Justice. "Last week," reported the left of center *Tablet* magazine in its June 30 issue:

> . . . the Department of Justice brought its first insurrectionist to justice. A 49-year-old Indiana grandmother of five, who walked into the Capitol Building through an open door on Jan. 6 and wandered around for 10 minutes, pleaded guilty

to "parading, demonstrating, or picketing in a Capitol building." For her crime, she was sentenced to three years of probation, $500 in restitution, and 40 hours of community service. Given that President Biden has called Jan. 6 the "worst attack on our democracy since the Civil War," how did she get off so easy? Her court-appointed lawyer had her read and watch *Bury My Heart at Wounded Knee*, *Just Mercy*, and *Schindler's List*, evidence that she was on her way to renouncing her white privilege. What does racism and exterminationist antisemitism have to do with the nonviolent crime she committed? Nothing, of course. The Biden administration sees Jan. 6 as a platform to criminalize its opponents, and the only way out for Donald Trump supporters is to confess to "thought crimes."[40]

Impeach Trump

For Trump, the path to absolution was not so easy. In fact, as far as Democrats were concerned, it was not possible at all. Five days after the January 6 break-in, Pelosi filed a single article of impeachment against Trump, charging him with "incitement of insurrection," which was introduced to the House of Representatives on January 11, 2021. It was Trump's second impeachment and the fourth in the entire history of the United States, which meant that he was the target of half of them. This was not only an abuse of power, but of the constitutional provision itself, which was not intended to be a weapon in the hands of a political faction.

The impeachment proceeding did not begin until the House impeachment managers formally delivered the charge to the Senate on January 25, five days after Trump had left office and Joe Biden had been inaugurated as America's forty-sixth president. In other words, Democrats were intent on removing a private citizen from an office he no longer held. This made no sense except as a perverse expression of their obsessive hatred of the man himself.

The transcript of Trump's January 6 speech was easily accessible on the internet, and not a single sentence could be interpreted as an incitement to any unlawful act, let alone "insurrection." Whether there were a million people gathered at the Ellipse to hear his "Stop the Steal" speech, as Trump claimed, or only 100,000 as the press reported, the number who breached the Capitol building that day was less than 1 percent of the total, making it hard to claim that anything that Trump said, which did not include attacking the Capitol, swayed his supporters. This was the point made by the alleged organizer of the break-in, Stewart Rhode, when he claimed that the actions of his militia members were a protest against what they perceived as Trump's inaction.

The team of House managers whom Pelosi had appointed to impeach Trump faced a seemingly daunting task. But Democrat imaginations, powered by an obsessive hate already racing ahead of any facts. Ironies abounded. For example, one of the House members selected by Pelosi to serve as a manager of the impeachment was Representative Eric Swalwell (D-California). Swalwell had been appointed by Pelosi to be the ranking member of the Intelligence Committee when he was still only a sophomore in the House. She had appointed him to such a sensitive position despite the fact that his rise to national prominence had occurred largely thanks to Christine Fang, a campaign bundler who U.S. intelligence officials "believed to have been acting at the behest of China's Ministry of State Security" [41] and with whom he reportedly was having a personal relationship; she fled the country when her cover was blown.

As a House prosecutor, Swalwell lost no time in seizing on the word *fight* in Trump's speech. He attempted to use the word to compare Trump to Osama bin Laden and the mini-riot of January 6 to the Islamic attacks of 9/11, a terrorist strike on New York City's Twin Towers and the Pentagon in Washington, D.C., that killed more than 3,000 people.

Swalwell's leaps of logic were a wonder to behold. "Osama Bin Laden did not enter U.S. soil on September 11," Swalwell told *PBS NewsHour*, "but it was widely acknowledged that he was responsible for inspiring the attack on our country and the president, with his words, using the word *fight*. . . . That is hate speech that inspired and radicalized people to storm the Capitol. . . . I'm comparing the words of an individual who would incite and radicalize somebody as Osama bin Laden did to what President Trump did. You don't actually have to commit the violence yourself, but if you call others to violence, that itself is a crime." [42]

Swalwell's attempt to criminalize Trump for invoking the word *fight* in this speech—a verb that politicians use all the time with nonviolent connotation—was widely ridiculed.[43] Yet in the surreal atmosphere of a Sovietlike show trial that surrounded the entire impeachment process, Swalwell's rhetorical absurdities had little effect on Pelosi's confidence in him or on her determination to put the now-private citizen Trump in the dock for a protest that he did not lead, and which was indisputably mild compared to the actual insurrections in American cities the previous summer that Democrats had generally supported. These leftist riots included numerous arson attacks on such symbols of law and authority as Federal buildings, the occupation and destruction of police precincts, setting fire to the historic Church of the Presidents in Washington, D.C., and the threatening of the White House itself. These criminal insurrections not only provoked no outrage among Democrats, but in fact garnered their support. Democrats regarded the perpetrators as "social justice warriors" and willingly bailed them out of jail.[44]

Trial by Diversion

To avoid the embarrassment of attempting to make the actual text of Trump's January 6 speech say what it clearly did not, the House impeachment managers, led by Representative Jamie Raskin, repeatedly asserted, without evidence, that merely by delivering an inflammatory speech and questioning the election procedures Trump had incited an attack on the Capitol. It was a claim that would have been thrown out of any real court on constitutional grounds alone.

Yet on December 11, Pelosi sent a "Dear Colleague" letter to the Democrats in the House, in which she said, "This week, 126 House Republicans, nearly two-thirds of the GOP Conference, signed on to an extreme partisan lawsuit demanding that the will of voters in four states—Georgia, Michigan, Pennsylvania, and Wisconsin—be overturned and that the Electoral College votes be awarded to Donald Trump. . . ."[45]

Pelosi simply ignored the possibility that there could have been organized irregularities corrupting the process. Those who claimed there were such irregularities were subversives seeking to overturn the election and destroy the Constitution: "As members of Congress, we take a solemn oath to support and defend the Constitution. Republicans are subverting the Constitution by their reckless and fruitless assault on our democracy, which threatens to seriously erode public trust in our most sacred democratic institutions."[46]

Pelosi also ignored the fact that the House Republicans were protesting the unconstitutional roles of Democrat courts, secretaries of state, governors, and attorneys general in changing the election laws. So did the House prosecutors who showed video clips of Trump's campaign speeches in which Trump questioned election procedures and the validity of changes in the rules. The Democrats then edited the videos of Trump's speeches so they were accompanied by footage of scuffles that Capitol police had with various fringe militia figures such as the Oath Keepers on January 6. In other words, with Raskin in the lead, the impeachment managers sought to make the mere act of questioning changes in election procedures an "insurrection" and, therefore, treason.

The Big Lie

In his testimony, Raskin described Trump's claim the election had been stolen as "the Big Lie that was responsible for inflaming and inciting the mob in the first place."[47] The phrase "Big Lie"— famously promoted as a political weapon in Adolf Hitler's *Mein Kampf*—became a mantra for Democrats seeking to make any questioning of the election result tantamount to the worst evil they could imagine. If any Republican suggested that the 2020 election might have been problematic, or defended Trump's criticism of it, Democrats dismissed them out of hand as repeating "the Big Lie," and therefore endangering the nation.[48]

Even before the formal impeachment process began, Representative Cori Bush submitted a resolution calling on the House Ethics Committee to investigate and expel the 139 House Republicans (later increased to 147) who supported Trump and voted to question the election result. Bush's resolution gained the support of 54 cosponsors, led by Alexandria Ocasio-Cortez and the leftist Squad in the House, and was accompanied by a petition in support of the resolution with 500,000 signatures. The resolution also described Representative Mo Brooks (R-Alabama) and Senators Ted Cruz (R-Texas) and Josh Hawley (R-Missouri) as leaders of "a politically motivated and last-ditch effort to overthrow the election." It also called on the House of Representatives to condemn the alleged disenfranchisement of black, brown, and indigenous voters, although minority Americans were actually voting in record numbers.[49] The irony that the leaders of the Squad who were making these demands were also supporters of Castro's Cuba—the longest surviving dictatorship in the hemisphere—went generally unmentioned.

Bush, a pro-Castro Marxist, had put forward her resolution on the day of the presidential election. Five days later, she tweeted: "Expel the Republican members of Congress who incited the white supremacist attempted coup."[50] The only evidence of white supremacy behind a nonexistent coup, however, was the fact that most of the crowd in the Capitol on January 6 were white.

In a normal world, Cori Bush would be dismissed as a fringe racist and Marxist throwback. But in the Democrat Party led by Biden and Pelosi, she was perfectly at home. Thus, Pelosi's choice to lead the House Managers prosecuting Trump was Jamie Raskin, a pro-Castro member of the Democratic Socialists of America and a lawyer who campaigned to give noncitizens and illegal aliens the right to vote in American elections.[51]

In January 2017, Raskin had led a delegation of leading Democrats—including Jim McGovern, Maxine Waters, Sheila Jackson Lee, Pramila Jayapal, and Barbara Lee—to the well of the House to challenge the Trump victory and call for the decertification of his electors.[52] In other words, in questioning and challenging the 2020 election result, Republicans were doing exactly what Democrats had done in 2017, after Trump's victory (and also in 2001, and 2005 after the Bush elections). But in their quest to hang Trump, congressional Democrats, with Raskin in the lead, ignored these facts and voted, to a person, to impeach Trump for doing the same thing.[53]

Erasing Trump and His Supporters

The improbable Senate impeachment trial of Trump began on February 9. He was acquitted four days later, as everyone knew he would be in the Republican-controlled chamber. Since the result was known in advance, the purpose of the "impeachment" was to tar and feather the former president who had received a record number of votes in the 2020 election and to tarnish his 74 million voters as supporters of a traitor.

Now Joe Biden was president and Trump was a private individual. For five years he had been the target of more defamatory attacks than perhaps anyone in history. Nonetheless, for the Democrats, this was still insufficient, and apparently would never be enough.

Just before the Senate vote, new Majority Leader Chuck Schumer publicly vowed that if the Senate convicted Trump, he would hold a vote to block Trump from ever holding public office again. The legal basis for such a ban would be a questionable interpretation of the Fourteenth Amendment, which was designed to prevent leaders of the Confederacy who had engaged in an armed rebellion from holding office in the government against whom they had declared war.

It was as though the Democrats had no filters for their Trump hatred, the relentless themes of whose presidency had been patriotic—to put "America First," and "Make America Great Again." Did they not think that the American public could put two and two together and realize the absurdity of their accusation that Trump was unpatriotic? Apparently not. Senator Tim Kaine filed his own resolution not only to censure Trump but to bar him, under the same clause in the Fourteenth Amendment, from ever holding public office again.[54]

Even that was not enough for Democrats on the warpath. Thirteen House Democrats sponsored a bill that would bar the federal government from naming any buildings or monuments after Trump and would also prevent him from being buried at Arlington National Cemetery.[55] Representative Linda Sánchez (D-California) went a step further and introduced a "No Glory for Hate Act" that would bar Trump from receiving his federal pension, office space, and paid staff, as other former presidents have. According to the *Washington Times*, Sánchez said Trump's name should not even appear on a park bench.[56] In Democrat-controlled New York City, ice-skating rinks that Trump had saved and built removed his name because of the opprobrium that Democrats and their supporting media had drummed up against him. Six "Trump Place" residential buildings dropped his name as well.[57]

The Democrats' obsession with erasing Trump was vindictive and petty, but it had a momentous political dimension. It wasn't Trump the Democrats feared most. It was the 74 million Americans who voted for him. Nine days after the January 6 protest, Representative Alexandria Ocasio-Cortez (D-New York) called on the federal government to fund the "deprogramming" of white supremacists and conspiracy theorists, a page straight out of the playbooks of Communist China and Soviet Russia.[58] It was classic totalitarianism 101: demonize your opponents so there is no legitimate opposition, only anti-Soviet traitors.

Drawing on the Cori Bush Black Lives Matter meme that January 6 was a "white supremacist coup," Ocasio-Cortez insisted that "[a] lot of people had drank[sic] the poison of white supremacy, and that's what Donald Trump represents."[59] She added: "The white supremacist cause is futile, it's nihilist. Their world will never exist. That's why we're seeing violence right now. . . . It's going to take a very long time to de-radicalize these people, and a lot of effort. This is a problem that doesn't go away on January 20 [Inauguration Day]."[60] In fact, according to Ocasio-Cortez, "healing" Trump supporters is possible only if "we . . . double, triple or quadruple the funds for these programs."[61] And, no doubt, adopt the coercive measures, like forced re-education camps, that would be necessary to get the Trump "cultists" to submit to their brainwashing. Obviously, winning electoral majorities was not even an option for dealing with such a diseased opposition. Only "de-programming" and "brainwashing" on a large scale might be up to the task.

As if the media were not mainly in the tank for the political left, Ocasio-Cortez also included this warning: "We're going to have to figure out how we rein in our media environment so that you can't just spew disinformation and misinformation."[62] This was a common theme of even "moderate" Democrats who felt that outlawing "misinformation" was required to right the ship of state. The president's fact-challenged Press Secretary, Jen Psaki, was constantly referring to this problem in a manner that was unfathomably tone deaf to historical tragedies and current political realities. During the election, the social media company Twitter had already deplatformed Trump even though he was a sitting president with 80 million Twitter followers. He was deplatformed because the Twitter executives didn't like his views and wanted Biden to win, and so suppressed them. They imposed the ban with hardly a Democrat in Congress or a so-called liberal in the media issuing a protest. In fact, many of them—including leading senators like Elizabeth Warren (D-Massachusetts) and California senator-turned-Vice President-elect Kamala Harris—had demanded it.

This was the problem dramatized by Ocasio-Cortez, a shallow communist and supporter of Palestinian terrorists with 8 million Twitter followers and an untoward impact on the Democrat Party leadership. Ocasio-Cortez's call for communist-like re-education camps was hardly unique among her Democrat colleagues. "No, seriously, . . . how *do* you deprogram 75 million people?" asked David Atkins, a California regional director of the Democratic Party. "We have to start thinking in terms of post-WWII Germany or Japan. Or the failures of Reconstruction in the South."[63]

Another communist, Nikole Hanna-Jones, an "investigative journalist" and the historically illiterate fabricator of *The New York Times' 1619 Project*, weighed in, telling Eugene Robinson of the *Washington Post* that the 74 million Americans who voted for Trump had to be "punished" for their vote and deprogrammed. To which Robinson concurred, saying, "There are millions of Americans, almost all white, almost all Republicans, who somehow need to be deprogrammed."[64] In fact, despite four years of being attacked by the Democrats and media as a "white supremacist" and a "racist," Trump had won 26 percent of the non-white vote, the second largest percentage of any Republican in the past hundred years.[65] So much for misinformation.

But the real support for the unhinged views of Cori Bush and Ocasio-Cortez came from the president-elect himself. Despite campaigning as a moderate and a "regular American," within days of taking office Joe Biden was revealing just how extreme his agenda actually was. A day after the January 6 protest, Biden introduced his pick for Attorney General, Merrick Garland, and said of the demonstrators, "Don't dare call them protesters. They were a riotous mob. Insurrectionists. Domestic terrorists. It's that basic. It's that simple."

Actually, not quite. Biden then blamed Trump for inciting the violence, saying he had "unleashed an all-out assault on our institutions of democracy. The past four years, we've had a president who's made his contempt for our democracy, our Constitution, and the rule of law clear in everything he has done."[66] Actually, it was more like Joe Biden who promised to govern as a centrist and a unifier and who had appointed to his national security team the very people who had fabricated the Russia-collusion hoax, who might fairly be described as someone "who had made his contempt for our democracy, our Constitution and the rule of law clear in everything he has done."

Based on the sketchy information available to Biden the day after the January 6 protest, his was a particularly warped view of the event, the crowd that participated in it, any role Trump may have had in it, and his general attitude toward civil disobedience, the Constitution, and the rule of law. From the May 25 death of George Floyd through Election Day, there had been at least 746 violent riots nationwide, 95 percent of which were conducted or led by Black Lives Matter,[67] an organization formally endorsed by the Democrat Party, and by Antifa, an armed communist militia whose declared purpose was to take the law into its own hands because government couldn't be trusted to know who the fascists were.[68]

During the Black Lives Matter/Antifa riots of 2020, federal buildings were torched, stores looted and destroyed, and individuals savagely beaten by mobs whose violence led to the defunding of police, a 62 percent rise in homicides of black people and the deaths of an estimated 2,000 inner city African Americans.[69] While Trump systematically called for law and order and sufficient force to stop them, Biden dismissed Antifa as merely "an idea,"[70] and said nothing when the federal agents Trump sent to defend federal court houses and buildings were denounced by Pelosi as "stormtroopers,"[71] while the criminal insurrectionists were bailed out of jail by the Minnesota Freedom Fund, an organization supported and promoted by the new vice president elect, Kamala Harris, and Biden's own staffers.[72]

By contrast, Trump's presidency was dedicated to putting "America First." This took many forms, including renegotiating trade deals unfavorable to the United States, destroying ISIS, and killing the leading anti-American terrorists Abu Bakr al-Baghdadi and General Qassem Soleimani (actions for which Trump was denounced by virtually all Democrats). Far from holding the Constitution in contempt, Trump had made defense of the First and Second Amendments, openly under attack by Democrats, a priority of his presidency. If Trump's political campaigns and agendas had a symbol, it was the American flag, which so-called progressives of Antifa and Black Lives Matter took pleasure in burning. If the Trump movement had a slogan to rally behind, it was "Make America Great Again." By any measure, Biden's characterizations of Trump were transparent and malicious lies. Or "misinformation" if one prefers.

Domestic Terrorists and Double Standards

The Democrats' partisan double-standard in administering justice was dramatized by Biden's appointee to head the Department of Justice. At his Senate confirmation hearing, the sixty-nine year old jurist Merrick Garland emphasized the Justice Department's responsibility to "battle extremist attacks on our democratic institutions" and described the January 6 event as "the most heinous attack on the democratic process" that he had ever seen.[73] Garland subsequently announced that the Justice Department was moving discretionary funds to address the problem and that the President's 2022 budget would "provide over $100 million in additional funds to address the rising threat of 'domestic violent extremism' and 'domestic terrorism,' including funding for the FBI, the U.S. Attorneys' Offices, the U.S. Marshals Service, and other components of the Department."[74]

During the Senate hearing over these priorities, Republican Senator Josh Hawley brought up the numerous, far more violent attacks that leftists had carried out against federal courthouses in Portland and Seattle during 2020.[75] Hawley then asked Garland: "Do you regard assaults on federal courthouses or other federal property as attacks of domestic extremism, domestic terrorism?"[76]

Garland replied that "an attack on a courthouse while in operation, trying to prevent judges from actually deciding cases, that plainly is domestic extremism, domestic terrorism. An attack simply on a government property at night or any other circumstances is a clear crime and a serious one and should be punished. I don't know enough about the facts of the example you're talking about, but that's where I draw the line. Both are criminal; one is a core attack on our democratic institutions."[77]

This specious distinction was a transparent attempt to exempt the left-wing rioters in Portland, Seattle, and other cities rent by their violence from being designated terrorists. This was despite the fact that Antifa and Black Lives Matter radicals had occupied and destroyed police stations—clearly an obstruction of the functions of the law on a par with attacking courthouses. In equating domestic terrorism solely with the actions of the political right,

as Biden and his minions did, Garland also overlooked
the mob invasion of the Senate confirmation hearings of
Justice Brett Kavanaugh in 2018. Led by Women's March
leader Linda Sarsour, the clear intentions of the intrusion
into government chambers, along with the outbursts that
followed, were to obstruct the hearings and prevent Kavanaugh's confirmation. The antics of Sarsour's mob led to
daily stoppages in the proceedings while the protesters—
several hundred all told—had to be arrested and removed
to allow the hearings to proceed.

Far from attacking the actions of these left-wing rioters,
the Democrats on the Judiciary Committee actually defended the disruptions. Senator Jeff Merkley (D-Oregon)
said, "It was a gutsy thing to do for women treated aw-
fully by powerful white men as if they are the problem
instead of an honest presenter of information."[78] In fact,
the mob's chants of "Women Rise Up!" had nothing to do
with presenting information, while the observation that
the Republican senators were white was only relevant as
an insight into the racism that had become normal for
Democrats on the attack.

Merrick Garland's entire answer to Senator Hawley's
pertinent question was a transparent dodge. If a courthouse is burned as the target of a protest, it sends a message: *If we don't like your decisions, we will attack you.* This is
an insurrectionary act against the processes of the law.
It is terrorism. The ubiquitous chant heard during the
Black Lives Matter and Antifa insurrections, looting, and
arsons—"No justice, no peace!"—is a terrorist threat: *Administer justice our way, or we will hurt you.* That is precisely

how terrorism works. And the problem remains that the routine terrorism of the left, its use of street violence as a means of political intimidation, is now sanctioned and supported by the highest levels of the Democrat Party.

The organizers of the January 6 break-in amounted to probably ninety-four individuals out of the 100,000 or so who attended Trump's "Stop the Steal" speech, although only forty-four were charged with conspiracy.[79] These individuals were already known and their agendas identified by law enforcement authorities. To attempt to equate the millions of Trump supporters with a fringe contingent of clearly identifiable radical groups may be politically useful to a party determined to criminalize its political opposition. But it has nothing to do with justice, or truth, or the constitutional principles that have made America the beacon of hope it has become for its own citizens and for people all over the world.

3

Inauguration

FOR MORE THAN four years, the focus of Democrat politics had been the demonization of Donald Trump and the effort to drive him out of public life. According to Democrats, Trump was an insensitive racist and a divider of the nation; he was uncompassionate and unpresidential, a xenophobe and a colluder with America's enemies, a traducer of the Constitution, a compulsive liar, an embarrassment to his high office, an un-American disgrace. In his campaign, Biden presented himself as an opportunity to escape from the dark cloud in which Trump was alleged to have engulfed the nation. Biden promised voters that he was the man to restore the optimism and unity of the American people. His presidency, moderate and tuned to American sensibilities, would make America normal again.

In his inauguration speech on January 20, Biden repeated this pledge: "Today, on this January day, my whole soul is in this: Bringing America together. Uniting our people. And uniting our nation. I ask every American to join me in this cause.[. . . Politics need not be a raging fire destroying everything in its path. . . . America has to be better than this." And then he promised: "I will be a President for all Americans. I will fight as hard for those who did not support me as for those who did."[1]

Every pledge Biden made in this speech was a lie. Biden had already prepared a series of executive actions that were unprecedented for their number and for their single unifying theme: to cancel or reverse, without public discussion or legislative input, the key policies of the Trump administration. In other words, Biden began his administration with a calculated stick in the eye of all 74 million Americans who had voted for Trump.

Biden's executive actions launched the most radical regime in American history, the very opposite of what he had promised voters during his presidential campaign. It announced that Biden was coming out as the leader of the radical left in his own party and would abandon all the promises of moderation he had made during his campaign.

In fact, there were two Biden campaigns: one to win over the radical left wing of his party in the primaries, and the other to seduce the moderate mainstream into thinking he was one of them. Biden's chief primary opponent was Senator Bernie Sanders (I-Vermont), a lifelong supporter of communist dictators and their monstrous regimes.

To radical Democrats Biden promised that he would be "the most progressive president in history."[2] On Inauguration Day he showed that was exactly what he intended to be.

The more than forty executive actions with which Biden began his presidency included stopping the construction of the southern border wall. This opened the southern border to what turned out to be an invasion by close to 2 million unknown and unvetted individuals from approximately 100 countries, including failed terrorist states. The border wall had been the centerpiece of Trump's campaign and tenure. It symbolized his determination to serve and protect the American people first. It also measured the degree to which the Democrat Party had detached itself from its principled past. Before Trump's campaign and presidency, Democrats had supported and funded the wall. Now they opposed it. They did so simply because Trump supported it. Stopping the wall endangered the security and lives of 330 million American citizens, but that didn't enter into the new Democrat calculus.

Equally disturbing to the Trump Republicans was Biden's Executive Action to have the United States rejoin the World Health Organization (WHO) from which Trump had withdrawn and to restore much of the nearly $500 million in funding for the WHO that Trump had cut off.[3] Trump had made these decisions when it was revealed that the WHO, which was controlled by China's Communist dictatorship, had colluded with the communists to conceal the contagious and deadly nature of the Covid-19 virus.[4]

In rescinding Trump's attempt to hold the pandemic spreaders accountable, and in restoring their authority and funding, Biden demanded no concessions from the Chinese. He simply acted as though Trump, rather than the Chinese Communists and their agents, was the problem.

A third Biden executive action restored hundreds of millions of dollars to Palestinian terrorists.[5] Trump had blocked these funds when the terrorist dictatorships in Gaza and the West Bank refused to stop using humanitarian and military aid to fund terror attacks on Jewish civilians. This Biden Executive Order brought to an end what was perhaps Trump's greatest foreign policy achievement: the Abraham Accords, which normalized relations between Israel and Muslim Arab nations that had been at war with the Jewish state for more than seventy years. It was the most promising development in Middle East peace efforts on record. But the Accords depended on an innovative policy—the isolation of the Palestinians, who for more than seventy years had refused to recognize the very existence of Israel or the use of terror to secure their goals. They rejected normalization because their clearly articulated, unwavering goal was Israel's destruction and the ethnic cleansing of its Jews—genocide.[6]

More than anything else, this reflected the radical nature of the new Democrat Party. The Squad members in the Party—Alexandria Ocasio-Cortez, Cori Bush, Ilhan Omar, Rashida Tlaib, Ayanna Presley, and Pramila Jayapal—were open supporters of the genocidal Hamas and Hezbollah terrorists and brazen purveyors of their genocidal lie that Israel occupied a state called Palestine when no such state ever existed and Israel was built entirely on land that belonged to the Turks—who were neither Palestinians nor Arabs—for 400 years before Israel's creation. Jordan, Lebanon, Syria, and Iraq were all created on the same Turkish land, but Cortez and her comrades had no objections to those states because they were not homelands of the Jews.

The Deepest Divide Is Race

As the very first of his priorities, only hours after his inauguration, Biden canceled the "1776 Commission" project Trump had launched at the very end of his term.[7] The decision reflected the fact that a clash between to two men and their parties over one issue—American patriotism—was greater and deeper than the border wall, the coronavirus, the Democrats' support for terrorists in the Middle East, or any other political difference that would shape the Biden presidency to come.

Trump formed the 1776 Commission by executive order on November 22, 2020, to oppose the *Times' 1619 Project,* which was designed to portray America as a white supremacist nation from its origins.[8] It sought to replace America's 1776 founding with the entirely unhistorical date of 1619, on which 20 alleged slaves arrived in the Virginia colony. The attack was led by the editorial board of America's "paper of record," *The New York Times,* whose editors explained its meaning in this statement:

> "The 1619 Project is a major initiative from *The New York Times* observing the 400th anniversary of the beginning of

American slavery. It aims to reframe the country's history, understanding 1619 as our true founding and placing the consequences of slavery and the contributions of black Americans at the very center of our national narrative."[9]

The *Times'* "reframing" of American history was based on a string of lies so obvious it was difficult to understand how the project's authors or Biden or the Democrat Party could give them credence. The United States of America, much less the state of Virginia, did not exist in 1619 when twenty Africans were shipped to the colony. So this was hardly the "beginning of American slavery," as the disingenuous editors of the *Times* maintained. In 1619, the United States would not exist for another 168 years. And it would only exist as the result of a revolutionary war dedicated to the proposition that all men had an "unalienable" right to liberty, a right that potentially included black slaves.

The 400-year time frame was a malicious invention of the political left and made sense only if the revolutionary acts that created an American identity were erased and the differences between Americans and their English colonial masters were conflated because both were white. The *Times'* version, in other words, depended on the racist view that race overrode every other aspect of human behavior.

The event the *Times* described as "the beginning of American slavery" was itself a fabrication. The twenty Africans were not slaves but indentured servants destined to work for five to seven years to pay off their passage to America and then be freed. The majority of the labor force in Virginia was composed of such indentured servants, and the majority of them were white.[10] Since all the slaves shipped to America were enslaved by black Africans and sold at slave auctions in Ghana and Benin, their enslavement had nothing to do with "American racism" but was the continuation of a practice that had existed in Africa for a thousand years before a white person ever set foot there.

As a result of efforts by the left-wing teachers unions, this calculated falsification of America's history was already part of the curriculum in thousands of American secondary schools by fall of 2020.

Trump created the 1776 Commission to defend the familiar historical narrative of America's past, its founding as a nation in a revolutionary war dedicated to the equality of all human beings and their unalienable right to be free. The commission's first report was issued two days before Biden's inauguration.[11]

The 1776 narrative included America's long commitment to creating a society of equals in which individuals were judged by their character and not their skin color. The words *white* and *black, male* and *female,* do not appear in the Constitution. America was not the invention of white supremacists, as the Biden radicals maintained. Unlike the *1619 Project*, the 1776 narrative was not created by partisan scholars. It had been established with research by tens of thousands of historians and scholars from all political sides over several hundred years.

In cancelling the 1776 Commission, Biden said that his administration would continue to push the anti-American curriculum in the schools and that there would be no 1776 curriculum to confront it with the facts. In April 2021, Biden's Education Department announced a "new grant priority for American History and Civics Education programs and cited the anti-racism activist Ibram X. Kendi and the *1619 Project*."[12]

The actual architect of the *1619 Project* is a journalist named Nikole Hannah-Jones who, beginning at age 19, has written articles about the "white race" as "barbaric devils" and "bloodsuckers."[13] Her influence is derived less from her own achievements than from the support she has garnered from cultural elites, led by *The New York Times*, the Pulitzer Foundation, the left-wing teacher unions and now the president himself. Despite fierce criticism from historians,[14] and against the advice of her own PhD fact-checker,[15] Hannah-Jones claimed in the lead article of the *1619 Project* that the American Revolution was fought primarily "to preserve the institution of slavery"[16] and that the U.S. Constitution is inherently racist, even though the Constitution makes no mention of race. It's true that the Constitution outlawed neither white indentured servitude nor black slavery as a compromise to gain the support of the Southern colonies. Yet even the abolitionist Frederick Douglass, himself a freed slave, asked, "If the Constitution were intended to be by its framers and adopters a slave-holding instrument, then why would neither 'slavery,' 'slave-holding,' nor 'slave' be anywhere found in it?"[17] In fact, the word *race* only first appeared in the Constitution with the 1870 passage of the Fifteenth Amendment, which said, "The right of citizens of the United States to vote shall not be denied or abridged by the United States or by any State on account of race, color, or previous condition of servitude."[18]

The historical reality is that America was the first nation in history dedicated to racial equality in principle, from its inception in 1776 to the passage of the Civil Rights Act of 1964, even though the persistence of racial prejudice and Jim Crow segregation in the South left the promise of 1776 not fully realized. Yet it's also true that the struggle to fulfill that promise has involved the sacrifice of hundreds of thousands of lives, both white and black, and trillions of dollars spent. To focus on America's racial flaws without also acknowledging her tremendous racial successes compared to other nations—not least the election of a black American as president and the enormous wealth and success of black celebrities—is both intellectually dishonest and politically unwise.

In abolishing Trump's 1776 Commission, Biden called it "offensive" and "counter-factual," typically empty claims.[19] His rejection of a narrative so central to America's self-understanding on the basis of no factual foundation was more than disturbing. For more than 250 years, the "Spirit of '76" had carried Americans through their greatest trials as they defended their country and expanded its freedoms. No less troubling was an American president's embrace of a fabricated history so racist and hostile to the nation, which he served as commander-in-chief. Worse, he had made clear in his inaugural statements that the indictment of America as a racist nation was going to be a central theme and organizing principle of his administration.

The Myth of Systemic Racism

"In my campaign for President," Biden said on January 26, "I made it very clear that the moment had arrived as a nation where we face deep racial inequities in America and . . . systemic racism that has plagued our nation for far, far too long."[20]

This was an embarrassing fiction. Nearly sixty years earlier, the historic Civil Rights Act outlawed systemic racism. If any American institution was systemically racist it would be subject to costly legal action and penalties. If "systemic racism touches every facet of American life," as Biden also claimed, there would be a tsunami of lawsuits and billions in settlements.[21] But there was no such tsunami, because the term "systemic racism" was just another myth created by the anti-American left to advance its radical agendas.

What sustained this fiction was the flawed and dangerous idea that in 2021, "disparities" in income or in representation in America were the result of discriminatory practices against races and genders rather than reflections of the talents of individuals and the choices they made. An African American had been elected president twice with the support of white majorities, while America's highest law enforcement posts, including its national security apparatus, were held by African Americans. No other country—black, brown, yellow, or white—could make that claim. Racial discrimination had been illegal for a generation, and by all social indicators any traces of it were rapidly receding into the past.

Too many African Americans were still poor and unable to sustain themselves without government help. But there was such help available. Moreover, since 80 percent of African Americans were not poor or on welfare, it was implausible to suggest without evidence that race and racism accounted for the plight of the other 20 percent.[22] Only by erasing the responsibility of individuals for their choices and actions was it possible to reduce people to their racial identities and claim that bigotry was the cause of disparity wherever it was found.

But that was exactly what Biden and the Democrats did. The idea that "white supremacy" is an accurate term to describe the nation, as they maintained, was utterly ridiculous—and worse. It could hardly be squared with the powerful cultural presence of African and Hispanic Americans, or their roles as sports and entertainment icons for America's youth of all shades and colors, or with their prominent offices in law enforcement and the military, or with the scarcity of discrimination lawsuits under the Civil Rights Act. Nor could a white supremacist America be squared with the fact that the highest-earning ethno-racial group was actually Asian Americans, with a median annual household income that was $20,000 higher than the corresponding figure for whites.[23]

How could that be the case in a society blighted by systemic racism, which was described as white supremacist?

Because America in 2021 was such a racially integrated and egalitarian society, and because racists were such an obviously marginal group, the left had developed an entire Aesopian vocabulary to obscure the fact that racism was already confined to a marginalized and insignificant social fringe. Terms such as *unconscious bias*, *implicit bias*, and *structural racism*, which for decades were mainly the purview of academia, came to the fore, deployed by the left to obscure the rarity of visible racists in the body politic and also to absolve supposed victim groups of responsibility for their circumstances.

Equity

The importance of these subterfuges became apparent as the Biden administration unveiled a new term to describe the central theme of its new policy agenda: equity. This buzzword quickly emerged as the guiding principle of the new administration's social and economic policies. On Inauguration Day, Biden issued an executive order outlining his agenda titled "On Advancing Racial Equity,"[24] which read, in part: "Equal opportunity is the bedrock of American democracy, and diversity is one of our country's greatest strengths. But for too many, the American Dream remains out of reach. Entrenched disparities in our laws and public policies, and in our public and private institutions, have often denied that equal opportunity to individuals and communities."[25]

But if there were actually "entrenched disparities" in American laws and policies resulting in discrimination against particular races and genders, they would be illegal. This made it clear from the outset that the new administration had no intention of dealing with actual denials of equal opportunity. It would instead implement a socialist vision in which government would redistribute income and privilege on the basis of gender and race. Mere disparities would become the unexamined rationale for this unconstitutional, unlawful, and anti-American redistribution of wealth by the Biden administration.

Biden's Executive Order continued: "Our country faces converging economic, health, and climate crises that have exposed and exacerbated inequities, while *a historic movement for justice* has highlighted the unbearable human costs of systemic racism" (emphasis added). This was a veiled reference to the Black Lives Matter Movement, a Marxist organization that was officially endorsed by the Democrat Party and which had allegedly helped raise $60 million for Biden's presidential campaign but produced no evidence for its claims of systemic racism and white supremacy and showed no interest in justice if the injustices were committed by blacks.

"Our Nation deserves an ambitious whole-of-government equity agenda that matches the scale of the opportunities and challenges that we face," Biden's order proclaimed. It went on to explain what "an ambitious whole-of-government equity agenda" meant. "It is therefore the policy of my administration that the Federal Government should pursue a comprehensive approach to advancing equity for all, including people of color and others who have been historically underserved, marginalized, and adversely affected by persistent poverty and inequality."

Biden's order then described the groups it intended to benefit with taxpayer dollars:

> For purposes of this order: (a) The term "equity" means the consistent and systematic fair, just, and impartial treatment of all individuals, including individuals who belong to underserved communities that have been denied such treatment, such as Black, Latino, and Indigenous and Native American persons; Asian Americans and Pacific Islanders and other persons of color; members of religious minorities; lesbian, gay, bisexual, transgender, and queer (LGBTQ+) persons; persons with disabilities; persons who live in rural areas; and persons otherwise adversely affected by persistent poverty or inequality.

Even this discriminatory list was dishonest. The Equity program was not for the "fair, just, and impartial treatment of all individuals." White Americans, including poor white Americans, were excluded. Asian Americans, the richest ethnic group in America, were treated as an economically oppressed minority because of their skin color. This was a socialist program for redistributing wealth on the basis of race and gender without regard to merit or actual "social injustice."

These realities were made clear by a billion-dollar equity program that had been authorized by Barack Obama and the Democrats as a payout to farmers living in rural areas—but only to those farmers who were non-white. This was an obvious violation of the Constitution's equal protection clause and of the Civil Rights Act of 1964. The Democrat Party was operating like the white supremacist Dixiecrats of the segregated South, but without the slightest self-awareness that they were.

Biden's $4 billion farm relief program to black farmers was a bid by the Democrats to sneak through a down payment on slavery reparations—156 years after the slaves were freed. Moreover, they were freed by the sacrifice of 350,000 mainly white lives and billions in treasure paid by the government from whom reparations were now being demanded. The subterfuge was necessary to pass reparations that were unpopular with a majority of Americans and, therefore, to do so without a vote. To accomplish the subterfuge, the Democrats included the anti-white farm relief program in a $1.9 trillion American Rescue Plan Act, which they billed as a pandemic-related stimulus legislation.

In its very first court test, the program was ruled unconstitutional because it was a clear violation of the equal protection clause. "The loan forgiveness program is based entirely on the race of the farmer or rancher," the judge wrote.[26] So central was the racist equity agenda to Biden's vision of the future that even before he formally took office, he announced his plan to administer Covid-19 relief on a racist basis.

"President-elect Joe Biden said this week that he will prioritize help for small businesses hurt by the Covid-19 pandemic based on the racial makeup and sex of their owners," KATV reported. Biden's own words: "Our focus will be on small businesses on Main Street that aren't wealthy and well connected, that are facing real economic hardships through no fault of their own. Our priority will be Black, Latino, Asian, and Native American owned small businesses, women-owned businesses, and finally having equal access to resources needed to reopen and rebuild."[27]

It was a repudiation of America's most essential value, enshrined in its birth certificate, which proclaimed "all men are created equal." Biden was letting the American people know that their new government would be guided by a vision in which "social justice" would be pursued through policies to redistribute income on the basis of skin color and politically correct gender status. These were policies antithetical to the principles that had inspired America's progress toward pluralism, diversity, and liberty for 250 years. In short, Biden intended to run the most overtly racist and anti-constitutional government in American history.

On the campaign trail, as rioters set fire to American cities and chanted "No Justice, No Peace," candidate Joe Biden had boasted on Twitter, "We're going to beat Donald Trump. And when we do, we won't just rebuild this nation—we'll transform it." By January 20, he already had.

4

Open Borders

O N JUNE 16, 1953, millions of East Germans rose up to protest the tyrannical Communist regime. In typical totalitarian-speak the Communist head of the Writers Union said that the people had forfeited the confidence of the government, when it was obvious that the reverse was true: the government did not have the confidence of the people. The uprising was ruthlessly crushed by Soviet tanks. To mark the event, the German poet Bertolt Brecht wrote a satirical poem offering advice to all tyrants impatient with the attitudes and values of the people they ruled. He called his poem "The Solution" and advised rulers who did not share their people's values, that rather than attempting to win their support it would be easier "to dissolve the people and elect another." This is probably the most insightful way to understand the new immigration policies that Joe Biden announced at his Inauguration.

The power of a nation to govern itself is made possible by enforceable borders. It is further secured by a citizenship process that requires immigrants to be educated in the nation's laws and customs, an oath of loyalty, and a pledge to assimilate to the values and traditions of the immigrant's new home.

It is a common mistake to think that the prosperity and freedoms of a nation are determined by economics, demography, sociology, or similar factors. In fact, a nation's success is determined by its culture. That is why a crowded island country with no natural resources, like Japan, is a prosperous first-world industrial power, while Mexico, a nation rich in natural resources, and independent for more than a century, is so mired in corruption, poverty and gang violence that more than a million of its inhabitants flee annually—and illegally—to the United States.

Democrats treat American citizenship, a concept that embodies the idea of a unique American identity, as disposable. That's why Democrats see no reason to exclude noncitizens from voting in American elections or receiving privileges like welfare, health care, and other government subsidies that American culture has made possible.[1] Democrats are wedded to an identity politics based on race. Making racial categories primary replaces the very idea of an American culture and identity and deprives its citizens of understanding the practices and principles that made their good fortune possible.

As believers in the primacy of race, Democrats view foreigners illegally crossing the southern border as "brown people" and therefore oppressed. But by whom are they oppressed? By a corrupt Mexican government run by brown people. According to Democrats, once these Mexicans cross the border they will be oppressed by America's systemic racism, which will be inflicted on them unconsciously by whites, who are rapidly becoming a minority in their own country—thanks to what? "White supremacists" who unconsciously oppress them, while inviting them into their country!

To Democrats, Americans who still believe in borders, citizenship, assimilation, and oaths of allegiance are racists, their good fortunes the ill-gotten gains of oppression. Three months into his administration, Biden banned the keywords *assimilation* and *illegal aliens* from the vocabularies of immigration officials. In their place, he substituted *integration* and *undocumented immigrants*, as though the problem of illegal immigration was one of lost papers and lack of inclusion.[2] The problem is *illegal* immigration, with no process of citizenship.

I Can't Legally Do This, But I Will

After his second election in 2012, President Barack Obama came under intense pressure from his radical base to declare an amnesty for the millions of people who had broken the law to cross anonymously into the United States. So great was the pressure from radicals that Obama was forced to publicly explain to them, at least twenty-two times, that the Constitution and subsequent statutory law prohibited him from declaring a general amnesty for people illegally residing in the United States.[3] Yet the prosperous, opportunity-rich country illegal immigrants were entering was actually created by these same constitutional limits to governmental authority.

"America is a nation of laws," Obama explained on one occasion, "which means I, as the President, am obligated to enforce the law. I don't have a choice about that. . . . With respect to the notion that I can just suspend deportations through executive order, that's just not the case, because they are laws on the books that Congress has passed. . . ."⁴ On another occasion he reminded people, "I swore an oath to uphold the laws on the books. . . ."⁵ And on yet another, he said: "Now, I know some people want me to bypass Congress and change the laws on my own. Believe me, the idea of doing things on my own is very tempting, I promise you. . . . But that's not how our system works. That's not how our democracy functions. That's not how our Constitution is written."⁶

When defending the American system suited his ends, Obama was a shrewd enough politician to understand its rationale and functions. But he himself was a born and bred radical, and as a radical didn't believe in the system itself or in the constitutional restraints the Founders created.⁷ For the same reason, his civics lectures fell on deaf ears. By their very nature, radicals reject the law and the constitutional order that supports it. That's what makes them radicals: their determination to change the legal system—not to obey or merely reform it.

On June 15, 2012, Obama did what he had repeatedly said the law and the Constitution barred him from doing. He issued an "executive branch memorandum" called the Deferred Action for Childhood Arrivals—DACA. This unilateral executive action provided a provisional amnesty for 600,000 youth who had entered the United States illegally as minors and were still under the age of 31 as of June 2012. DACA allowed these individuals to gain temporary legal status, work permits, access to publicly funded social services, and protection from deportation.⁸ All of which were both un-Constitutional and illegal.

Two years later, having witnessed scant resistance from Republicans and having gotten away with his illegal action, Obama decided to expand the scope of his crime. He undertook a second executive action, this time granting provisional amnesty to 4 million illegal aliens under the Deferred Action for Parents of Americans and Lawful Permanent Residents (DAPA) program—an expansion of DACA.[9]

Like DACA, this new executive order was unconstitutional and unlawful. Both were gifts to the criminal cartels who make millions of dollars trafficking exploited and desperate migrants across the border and to the enormous constituencies of Mexicans and Central Americans, who wanted to come to America for the opportunities it offered.

The illegal executive orders provided the victorious 2016 Republican presidential candidate, Donald Trump, with his principal campaign theme: "We're going to build a wall. We're going to have strong, incredible borders. And people are going to come into our country, but they're going to come in legally."[10] For the next four years Democrats waged a relentless war against Trump, his border wall, and his border security policies.

Trump's success in defending America's borders and constitutional order could be measured in the decline of the number of apprehensions of illegal migrants along America's southwest border. After peaking at 144,116 apprehensions in May 2019—that was in just one month, and not counting the large numbers who were never caught—the total number of apprehensions declined

precipitously each and every month for the rest of the year.
By December 2019, the total apprehensions had declined
to just 40,565. By April 2020, the figure had declined to
just 17,106.[11] In other words, Trump's policies—however
imperfectly implemented—had reduced apprehensions of
illegal aliens attempting to sneak across the border by 88
percent from the peak.

The Anti-Trump President in Action

After the 2020 election was decided against Trump, Joe
Biden launched his new administration with executive
actions whose common theme was repealing Trump's key
policies—especially his border policies—without regard to
their merits or the predictable consequences of abandoning them.

Among the first of Biden's actions was stopping construction of the border wall itself. Even the title of Biden's
order was written as a pointedly anti-Trump message:
"Presidential Proclamation on the Termination of Emergency with Respect to the Southern Border of the United
States and Redirection of Funds Diverted to Border Wall
Construction."[12]

In other words, Biden was saying that by proclamation
he was terminating the emergency at the border by undoing all the measures Trump had taken to secure it. "Building a massive wall that spans the entire southern border
is not a serious policy solution. It is a waste of money that
diverts attention from genuine threats to our homeland
security." This justification for the stoppage was absurd

on its face, as the flood of illegals crossing into the United States through gaps in the wall that Biden was refusing to close made rapidly evident. It was hypocritical as well. Before Trump made the importance of completing the wall the centerpiece of his presidential campaign in 2015, the congressional Democrats—with the support of President Obama and Vice President Biden—had voted to build the wall and to fund it.

Like a deluded dictator, Biden had proclaimed the border problem "terminated" by his word alone.[13] Biden and the Democrats simply did not, and do not, regard the lawless invasion of the country by unknown foreigners who include criminal cartel members, sex traffickers, drug dealers, and terrorists as a problem.

Nor did the Democrats see anything wrong with Biden's decision to make transformative changes in national policy without consulting Congress, or attempting to forge a bipartisan consensus on so momentous a change to existing law, precedent, and constitutional arrangement. After Trump was elected president by a narrow margin in 2016, Democrats complained that he had "no mandate" for any of the policies they disagreed with. Biden had been elected by a miniscule margin—.027 percent of the vote. It was one of the narrowest margins in the history of presidential elections. But that was no problem for Biden, or for his Democrat colleagues, when it came to dismantling major border policies that had brought illegal border violations dramatically down.

Biden's unilateral actions on Inauguration Day posed serious dangers to American citizens. This was highlighted by his decision to cancel one of Trump's first acts in office, which was to make a priority of deporting all illegal aliens who were guilty of other criminal acts. Trump's order was called "Enhancing Public Safety in the Interior of the United States." In addition to making the deportation of criminals a priority, the Trump policy also undid Obama's unconstitutional immigration orders, which exempted nearly all resident illegals from removal. It also made the 500 or so Democrat-run sanctuary cities, which were in open rebellion against existing U.S. immigration laws ineligible for federal grants, except those deemed necessary for law enforcement.[14] Biden's Inauguration Day orders unilaterally rendered these Trump policies null and void.

Another casualty of Biden's early anti-Trump actions was his withdrawal from the "Remain in Mexico" program, which Trump had negotiated with Mexico to force illegal asylum-seekers to wait in that country for their cases to be resolved. This had a major impact on the flow of illegal migrants attempting to enter the country anonymously and without undergoing a citizenship process.[15]

Over the next four months, Biden issued 94 executive orders on immigration policy, reversing 62 of Trump's orders and completely undoing the reforms that Trump had put in place to make the borders more secure.[16] Under the new orders, violent criminals who committed their felonies years earlier would now be eligible to remain in the United States instead of being deported. Ordinary criminals would no longer be eligible for deportation unless they had committed aggravated felonies, and then only if they were determined to be a threat to public safety and had no mitigating factors to earn them sympathy, such as "personal and family circumstances," and "health and medical factors."[17]

In keeping with these policies designed to protect criminals who were in the United States illegally, Biden cancelled Trump's order that the Department of Homeland Security provide periodic reports on the crimes illegal aliens committed.[18] Consequently, the public was generally unaware of the threat these new policies posed. According to the Libertarian CATO Institute, in 2017 there were 106,432 illegal aliens in prison for felonies they had committed while in the United States.[19]

In September 2015, Fox News reporter Malia Zimmerman revealed that government statistics showed illegal immigrants constituted just over 3 percent of the U.S. population but represented 13.6 percent of all offenders sentenced for crimes committed in the United States, including 12 percent of murder sentences, 20 percent of kidnapping sentences, and 16 percent of drug trafficking sentences.[20]

According to political analyst Peter Gemma, "75 percent of those on the most wanted criminals list in Los Angeles, Phoenix, and Albuquerque are illegal aliens" and "one quarter of all inmates in California detention centers are Mexican nationals, as are more than 40 percent of all inmates in Arizona and 48 percent in New Mexico jails." Moreover, 53 percent of all investigated burglaries reported in California, New Mexico, Nevada, Arizona, and Texas are perpetrated by illegal aliens.[21]

Other studies confirm these grim statistics. A 2018 report by the Government Accountability Office (GAO) stated that while illegal aliens compose about 3.3 percent of the U.S. population, they accounted for some 21 percent of all federal prison inmates. "And the actual picture may be worse," wrote Sharyl Atkisson in *The Hill*, "since the government says it has no way to be notified of all imprisoned illegal immigrants. So, instead, it counts a subset of them that it learns about through identifiers such as an FBI number." The GAO study found that between 2011 and 2016, there were more than 730,000 aliens in U.S. or state prisons and local jails, accounting for 4.9 million arrests for 7.5 million offenses. Their offenses included more than 1 million drug crimes, as well as roughly 500,000 assaults, 133,800 sex offenses, 24,200 kidnappings, 33,300 homicide-related events, and 1,500 terrorism-related crimes.[22]

Yet the new Biden administration regarded these statistics as insignificant, or, more likely, easy to hide from the American public. The absence of reporting on these facts affecting ordinary Americans protected the Biden administration from public outrage when habitual criminals, let in by their irresponsible policies, claimed more victims among America's law-abiding and vulnerable citizens.

On January 20, 2021, his first day in office, Biden sent Congress a comprehensive immigration bill—the U.S. Citizenship Act of 2021—proposing major overhauls to America's immigration system, codifying his open-border policies, and granting amnesty to 14.5 million people

already illegally in the country.[23] The bill even encouraged illegal aliens who had been deported by the Trump
administration to reapply for citizenship. This was a slan-
derous insinuation against Trump officials, who annually
approved the legal immigration of more than a million
people of diverse nationalities and races, that they were
racist, xenophobic, and biased against foreigners.[24]

Trump's immigration policy adviser, Stephen Miller, denounced the Biden proposal and the immigration revolution it represented in these chilling terms: "It is the most
radical immigration bill ever written, ever drafted, ever submitted in the history of this country," he said. "It is breath-
taking. It is a full-scale attack on the very idea of nationhood.
If you were trying to write a bill to eliminate the concept of
having a nation, this is the bill you would write."[25]

Multiple Consequences

Through his immigration decrees and encouragements to
illegal aliens, Biden obliterated America's borders—both
literally and in the minds of millions of impoverished
or criminal individuals in Latin America and all over the
world. It was a nation-altering act accomplished in the
most undemocratic way possible—without a congressional debate or a national consensus as to what America's border policy should be. Equally incomprehensible,
Biden did all this without any plan for what his administration would do to avoid the predictable humanitarian
crisis that a surge of illegal border crossings was bound
to create.

In October 2020, the last month before Biden's election, the number of apprehensions of illegals at the border was approximately 69,000.[26] In February 2021, one month into the new Biden policies, the number rose to 100,441, which was followed immediately by a series of escalating record highs: 173,337 in March; 178,854 in April; 180,034 in May; 188,829 in June; and 212,672 in July.[27] The latter was the largest number the nation had seen in any month since the creation of the Department of Homeland Security in 2002.[28] Meanwhile, unaccompanied minors were likewise responding to Biden's irresponsible invitations to come to the United States. They were doing so in unprecedented numbers: 18, 877 in March, and more than 19,000 in July.[29]

The monthly number of illegal border crossers was particularly remarkable in light of the fact that border arrests in the past had typically decreased during the brutally hot summers. For example, the border apprehension total for June in Trump's last year was 33,049, about one-sixth of the Biden total in June 2021.[30] The record figures from 2021 included unaccompanied minors, families, and individuals who gave themselves up to Border Patrol because the new Biden policy promised them permanent residency and eventual citizenship and benefits like welfare and free medical care. But even these figures did not include the estimated 30,000 individuals—including unknown numbers of criminals, terrorists, sex traffickers, and drug runners—who, each and every month, evaded capture and entered the country undetected.[31]

While these record numbers were piling up, and despite the fact that the migrants were packed into inadequate holding centers where diseases were rife and sexual abuses of women and children disturbingly frequent, the Biden administration refused to address it as the emergency it was. The chorus of complainers from the congressional "Squad" about child abuse when Trump was president was silent. And unlike Trump, who reversed the "zero-tolerance" policy within two months, the Biden White House attempted to hide the facts, stonewall its critics, and maintain that what was taking place was not actually a crisis but a "challenge." Instead of taking actions to alleviate the suffering, the Biden team issued orders barring the press from entering or photographing the facilities, and thus revealing to the public the extent of the damage their policies had caused.

Suffer the Little Children

This dereliction of government duty was particularly notable since the Democrats had lost no time in portraying Trump as a heartless monster for allegedly separating migrant children from their parents. The situation that had outraged Democrats was Trump's attempt to stem the flow of illegals with a "zero-tolerance" policy for anyone entering the country illegally. This had the ancillary effect of separating children from their parents, since it was U.S. policy not to incarcerate children when their parents committed crimes.[32]

The spaces the children were held in were enclosed by chain-link fences that had been built under the Obama administration. During Obama's tenure, there were no complaints from Democrats about these facilities. But with Trump in the White House, the Democrats, led by the Ocasio-Cortez radicals, had no compunction about calling them "cages" and comparing them to Nazi concentration camps.[33] "Let's talk about what we're talking about," an outraged Biden said about Trump's zero-tolerance policy for illegal adults during the presidential debates. "What happened? Parents were ripped—their kids were ripped from their arms and separated, and now they cannot find over 500 sets of those parents and those kids are alone. Nowhere to go. Nowhere to go. It's criminal. It's criminal."[34]

Parroting Biden, Senator Bernie Sanders excoriated Trump: "You don't rip little children away from the arms of their mother," although this was the standard policy for children of parents who had committed crimes under all presidents, Democrats and Republicans. Senator Elizabeth Warren expressed her disgust by adding another canard to her attack: "President Trump seems to think *the only way to have immigration rules* is [to] rip parents from their families . . . and to put children in cages"[35] (emphasis added).

The problem with the Democrats' outrage was that the photographs of the children in cages, splashed across the covers of innumerable magazines and aired nightly on TV news broadcasts, were actually taken in 2014, when Obama was still president.[36] In other words, it was

Obama's policy that had caged minor children in those so-called Nazi concentration camps, albeit along with their parents, and it was Obama who provided the facilities for their confinement.[37,38] But, as usual, rhetoric prevailed over reality, and the hue and cry Democrats raised was so great, and their refusal to negotiate a sensible border policy so firm, that Trump decided to end the policy only two months after he initiated it. "I didn't like the sight or the feeling of families being separated," he explained. Trump's order also required the Defense Department to construct facilities in which to house and care for the reunited families.

With their outcries, the Democrats won the battle to gain entry for adults coming into the country illegally—provided they were accompanied by children. But even after Trump had given the Democrats their victory, his concession didn't prevent them from continuing their campaign of character assassination, portraying him as a Nazi who happily ripped children from their mothers' arms. Among Biden's initial executive orders was one to create a "Task Force on the Reunification of Families," which went out of its way to strike an additional blow at Trump for his alleged cruelty. In the words of the order: "My administration condemns the human tragedy that occurred when our immigration laws were used to separate children from their parents or legal guardians (families), including through the use of the Zero-Tolerance Policy."[39]

With this order, Democrats went back to their posture of ignoring the suffering their own policies caused and the reality that their policies actually encouraged unaccompanied minors to flood across the southern border into the United States.[40] To give some context: *The Hill* described the journey from Central America and Mexico to the United States, which could be as long as 1,000 miles, as "one of the most dangerous trips in the world."[41] In a report documenting the conditions of migrants along that route between 2018 and 2020, Doctors Without Borders noted that of illegals who were questioned by border authorities about their experiences along the migration route, 57 percent reported that they had been victims of some type of violence.[42]

Yet despite this, Biden and members of his administration decided to make statements and implement policies that encouraged rather than discouraged parents to send their children alone, or in the custody of paid human traffickers, on this dangerous, potentially life-threatening journey. While Biden's statement that "no unaccompanied migrants under the age of 18 will be turned away at the border"[43] sounded compassionate at first, the consequence of this overt change in official U.S. policy was that tens of thousands of minor children would make the dangerous journey north who might not have done so without the explicit guarantee, from the president of the United States, that they could enter the country no matter what.[44]

It's true that in the last months of Trump's term, the number of unaccompanied children in the care of Health and Human Services was climbing steadily each month: 1,929 in October; 2,397 in November; 3,691 in December;

4,020 in January. But once Biden took office and announced that no child would be turned away from the U.S. border, those numbers predictably rose sharply. By February 2021, just a month after Biden's executive order went into effect, the number of unaccompanied children in the custody of Health and Human Services had more than doubled, to 6,581. In March, the figure had grown to 20,339. This was nearly eight *times* the average number under Trump.[45] And despite a dip over the summer months (possibly due to decreased numbers of migrants overall during the oppressive, often life-threatening heat), the number continued to hover between 12,000 and 16,000 per month in the fall of 2021.[46] Yet no cries of anguish were heard from Bernie Sanders, Elizabeth Warren, and the Democrats who had been so horrified by the former president's two-month zero-tolerance policy.

The ordeal that migrant children suffer after crossing the border and being placed in detention centers is only exacerbated by the effects of communicable diseases that spread like wildfire in the Biden administration's cramped, overcrowded detention facilities—the result of opening the border without planning for the inevitable influx of migrants.[47] In a sampling of girls at one temporary shelter for migrant teenagers in San Diego, for instance, nearly 10 percent tested positive for Covid-19. Similarly, 11 percent to 14 percent of migrant children at a facility in Carrizo Springs, Texas, tested positive. In May, Health and Human Services reported more than 3,000 coronavirus cases among migrant children in Texas.[48]

Yet no one cared. The corporate media was silent. To the Democrats, opening the U.S. border was what mattered—not the suffering it caused those who heeded their numerous invitations to come.

Of course, "opening the border" meant that it was now controlled by Mexican drug cartels. The minors unaccompanied by their parents were shepherded by ruthless cartel smugglers who charged their parents as much as $15,000 per trip—half on embarking and half on arrival. Failure to pay the second half was punished by brutal executions. The anguish of the young migrants was reflected movingly in the video of a terrified, sobbing 10-year-old Nicaraguan boy who was found and rescued by Border Patrol agents after having been abandoned by a larger group of migrants in the vast and desolate Rio Grande Valley.

That parents would expose their children to such risks might seem inexplicable. Yet the risks may have seemed worth it because once their children crossed the border, the new Biden orders would immunize them from deportation. Then "family reunification" would secure a free pass for the adults connected to them as the result of a policy often called "chain migration," which allows relatives to follow once illegal aliens gained a legal foothold on U.S. soil.[49]

The chief beneficiary of Biden's border policies were the Mexican cartels, whose smuggling, sex trafficking, and drug trade operations brought in wealth greater than that of many countries.[50] By one count, the cartels' operations were bringing in an estimated $500 billion annually.[51] What's more, the flood of human trafficking following

Biden's election caused cartel revenues to "skyrocket," according to a report by CBS News in June 2021: "We are seeing that the cartels are exploiting our current influx of unaccompanied children as well as our influx of single adults, and they're bringing hard drugs," U.S. Border Patrol agent Joel Freeland told reporter Janet Shamlin. According to Freeland, Shamlin said, "U.S. manpower focused on human smuggling is enabling traffickers to move a staggering amount of drugs."[52]

By July 6, 2021, Customs and Border Protection agents had already seized 8,507 pounds of fentanyl since the beginning of the fiscal year. This was 78 percent more than the 4,776 pounds they had seized in all of FY 2020.[53] The life-and-death implications of these figures are impossible to overstate. Fentanyl is 80 to 100 times as strong as morphine, meaning that a single pound of fentanyl can potentially kill more than 226,000 people.[54] Thus, the amount of fentanyl seized by border agents just between January and April 2021 would have been enough to kill nearly 1.5 billion people—or more than four times the entire population of the United States. Dr. Darien Sutton, a Los Angeles–based physician and ABC News contributor, summarized the potential impact: "When you talk about that amount, how many communities and people that will be affected and how many deaths that will be associated with it, you can't even comprehend it just because it's not fathomable."[55]

As *spectator.org* noted, "the majority of the fentanyl brought into the U.S. is not seized, and increasing amounts . . . are reaching Americans."[56] In 2020—before

President Biden's policies had made the U.S. border porous and unsecured, drug-related overdose deaths already totaled approximately 93,000.[57] About 60 percent[58] of those, or 55,800, were due to fentanyl—meaning that, on average, more than 150 people died of fentanyl overdoses each and every day in the United States.

Importing the Virus

Amid these staggering numbers, the White House doubled down on its refusal to complete the wall that Trump had begun, which would have stopped the flow of cartel-chaperoned children and adults at the border itself. Their refusal was active, not just passive. On June 11, 2021, the Associated Press reported: "Biden plans to return more than $2 billion that the Trump administration diverted from the Pentagon to help pay for the wall and use other money appropriated by Congress to address 'urgent life, safety, and environmental issues' created by the construction. [The President's plan] also asks lawmakers not to provide any additional funding for what the Biden team believes is an unnecessary effort."[59] According to Biden's team, the wall was the problem, not the catastrophic effects of failing to complete it.

Yet despite the Biden White House's continuing efforts to hide what was happening at the border, reports began to circulate as members of Congress began visiting the detention facilities and saw the squalid conditions with their own eyes. As a result, two months into his administration, Biden appointed Vice President Kamala Harris to take charge of the border crisis. Yet over the coming months, Harris did nothing. In fact, her failure to even visit the border became a national joke, ridiculed in hundreds of YouTube videos.

Finally, on June 25, after Donald Trump announced that if Harris would not visit the border, then he would, she reluctantly made a perfunctory trip. Even then, Harris chose to visit the well-secured processing center in El Paso on the border with New Mexico rather than a place where illegal border crossings were completely out of control—like McAllen, Texas, 769 miles away from the processing center that Harris visited. In fact, Harris never did make it to the actual border. Instead, she lectured the country endlessly about what she called the "root causes" of the crisis—the corrupt and impoverished societies the migrants came from, which had been impoverished and corrupt for 100 years.[60]

While Kamala Harris turned dereliction of duty into an art form, the Biden administration continued to bar media from accessing any of its chaotic, disease-ridden processing centers. For many weeks, federal agencies refused or ignored dozens of news media requests for access to those sites.[61] And even when the administration finally allowed reporters to enter one Texas border facility for the first time on March 24, it continued to prevent them from getting anywhere close to facilities that were filled far above their capacities in order to assess the suffering that the current policies were causing.[62]

In their continuing opposition to any meaningful border security, let alone a border wall, the Biden team revealed a callousness toward human suffering that was distinctly un-American and hard to understand. It underscored the obvious hypocrisy of the Democrats, who exaggerated the two-month crisis caused by Trump's zero-tolerance policy, which he then cancelled. More importantly, it revealed how completely Biden's border policies were driven both by anti-Trump hatred and by the Democrats' decades-long desire to change the demographics of the voting population rather than offer any practical solution to the border problem.

How could this president blow up the southern border in the face of a global pandemic that was entering a new phase as the result of new variants and mutations? During the campaign and his presidency, Biden has repeatedly presented himself as the nation's savior from the coronavirus pandemic. In the presidential debates, he accused Trump of killing every victim of the virus through incompetence, inaction, and sheer malice. But once in office, Biden took credit for Operation Warp Speed, Trump's record-setting initiative to mass-produce a Covid-19 vaccine, the only identifiable federal action that could be said to have turned the pandemic's tide.[63]

On Inauguration Day 2021, with one of his very first executive orders, Biden set out to dismantle America's southern border, heedless of the consequences. His abruptly cancelling Trump's border-security measures created a situation in which an estimated 1.7 million unvetted and untested illegal migrants were able to disappear into the United States in the first seven months of 2021.[64]

As NBC News reported, testing of several cohorts of illegal migrants apprehended at the border found that 18 percent of migrant families—and up to 20 percent of unaccompanied migrant children—tested positive for COVID on leaving Border Patrol custody.[65] The reality, however, is that many if not most migrants caught entering the United States illegally are not even tested, often only those showing symptoms. Migrants dropped off at bus stations by Border Patrol agents "are likely not tested before they leave to other cities," conceded *Newsweek*'s fact-checking department. "There is currently no system in place to keep track of whether migrants get tested for COVID-19 once they leave DHS custody."[66] Thus, while U.S. citizens must show proof of a negative PCR test within the past one to three days[67] before being allowed into their own country, migrants caught entering the country illegally, under the Biden administration's rules, usually do not.[68]

Of course, Democrats were quick to claim that even to mention this fact is racist, because a century ago nativist U.S. politicians claimed that poor immigrants, such as the Italians and the Irish, were potential carriers of disease.

What's more, the Biden administration went out of its way to waive Covid-19 testing and other restrictions for the illegal aliens, helping them to disappear into the interior without regard for the health and safety of the unsuspecting Americans they encountered. In other words, aside from China's original disinformation about the origins of the virus and its lethal nature, Biden's executive orders were the most reckless, irresponsible, and deadly actions taken in the course of a pandemic that had already ended 700,000 American lives.

Replacing the Population

By the middle of 2021, it was clear that the Biden administration was determined to keep the southern border open despite the catastrophic consequences and human suffering it caused. Biden and his cabinet focused their energy on appearances, directing their attention away from the eyesore that was the border itself and onto their agenda of changing the voting demographics of the nation.

To accomplish this, Biden enlisted the U.S. military, using Laughlin Air Force Base in Texas as a launching point for the administration's plan to secretly transport unvetted and un-tested illegal migrants to locations across the United States. This story first came to light in July 2021, when a whistleblower revealed to Fox News anchor Tucker Carlson that Lieutenant Colonel Matthew Burrows, who was stationed at Laughlin, had recently sent his subordinates an email that revealed the extent of the secret transport operation. "Over the next few days, weeks, or months [. . .] you may see passenger aircraft on our ramp transporting undocumented non-citizens," Burrows's email said. "Do not take photographs, and refrain from posting anything on social media." Army Lt. Col. Chris Mitchell, a spokesman for the Department of Defense, subsequently confirmed that such flights were indeed occurring as part of a "noncitizen movement" initiative.[69]

Prominent among the destinations for the migrants were states Democrats were targeting in their election campaigns—Florida, Michigan, North Carolina, Georgia, Kentucky, and Texas. In his report, Carlson noted the obvious: The Biden administration was using the U.S. military not for the defense of the country against foreign enemies but to assist in the task of "changing the electoral map" and enacting "demographic transformation in our country, without our consent, and in violation of our laws."[70]

Former Trump White House adviser Stephen Miller put it this way: "[W]hat is happening now is unprecedented. . . . This is not about an administration that is unable to protect the border. This is about an administration that in a very purposeful, planned, deliberate, painstaking fashion has turned our Border Patrol and ICE agencies into resettlement agencies. . . . This is a planned resettlement."[71]

Behind this mass resettlement lay a number of undisputed political facts. Approximately 70 percent of Hispanic voters in the United States today cast their ballots for Democrats.[72] This is consistent with a Pew Research Center finding that 75 percent of Hispanics in America would prefer a bigger federal government that provides more taxpayer-funded services—a typically Democrat position—as compared to just 41 percent of the overall U.S. population.[73]

As *The Washington Times* summarized: "With declining support from white and older Americans, the Democrats have concluded that their future lies in importing a new electorate from south of the border." This agenda was confirmed by the many unsolicited comments and efforts of the Democrats to blur the distinction between citizens and noncitizens by giving welfare and other benefits to anyone physically within U.S. borders and to drop the citizen requirements for voting.

The notion that Democrats and their supporters in the government have long sought to alter the demographic makeup of the United States has been an open fact in Washington for decades. It is a secret that Democrats themselves openly discuss among themselves—celebrating the rapid decline in the native-born U.S. population—and decry as racist whenever Republicans and others notice it.

That political power, and not some high-minded commitment to diversity as a political principle, is motivating the Democrats' push for demographic transformation was highlighted in July 2021. In that month, mass protests erupted against the 62-year-old communist dictatorship in Cuba. Five months earlier, Homeland Security Secretary Alejandro Mayorkas assured young people in Mexico and Central America that the new American regime would welcome them if they managed to cross the border illegally: "We well understand that out of desperation, some . . . loving parents might send their child to traverse Mexico alone to reach the southern border—our southern border. I hope they don't undertake that perilous journey. But if they do, we will not expel that young child. We will care for that young child and unite that child with a responsible parent. That is who we are as a nation and we can do it."[74]

Not so the Cubans. In a July 13, 2021, press conference at the U.S. Coast Guard Headquarters, Mayorkas slammed the door on would-be Cuban refugees in no uncertain terms: "The time is never right to attempt migration by sea. To those who risk their lives doing so, this risk is not worth taking. Allow me to be clear: If you take to the sea, you will not come to the United States."[75]

Why the change of tone, particularly since the Democrats' case against Trump was that America was a "nation of immigrants" and a sanctuary for immigrants seeking refuge? Perhaps because Cubans in the United States have a history of supporting Republicans,[76] while Hispanic Americans from Mexico, Puerto Rico, Guatemala, and other Central American countries vote in 70 percent majorities for Democrats. The only sympathy-driven ambivalence the Democrats displayed toward the Cubans was directed toward the oppressive regime that had bankrupted the country and turned it into an island prison. It took Biden a full week to decide on a hostile stance toward a sadistic regime and its people crying out for freedom.

In 1970, the population of California was 90 percent "non-Hispanic whites," according to the U.S. Bureau of the Census. It was the California of the Beach Boys and technology start-ups, of *American Graffiti* and Jonas Salk. At that time, California led the United States in education, economic output, and innovation—and voted consistently Republican. In fact, Republicans won the state in nearly every presidential election between 1952 and 1988.[77] Both Ronald Reagan and Richard Nixon were California politicians.

Yet after fifty years of massive legal and illegal immigration, primarily from Mexico, California's population has been completely transformed. It is now the multicultural paradise that Democrats have long worked to achieve: 39 percent Latino, 36 percent non-Hispanic white, 15 percent Asian, and 6 percent Black (down from 1970).[78]

The Democrats' plan worked: Because Latinos and Asians vote overwhelmingly for Democrats, California is now a one-party state in which Democrats control virtually all state executive offices. The Democrats took over the state by replacing the non-Hispanic white population with voters more supportive of their policies.

Not coincidentally, California now leads the country not in innovation but in dysfunction: along with the country's largest immigrant population, it now has the highest poverty rate in the country, ahead of Mississippi and West Virginia.[79] The United Nations compared the tent encampments of San Francisco to the slums of New Delhi and Mexico City.[80]

The once golden state now has the largest number of chronically homeless people in America[81] and is now home to one-third of the people across the entire country who are on welfare.[82] Once the pride of the nation for its schools and universities, California now holds the distinction of being the least-educated state in America with the highest number of high school dropouts.[83]

In 2019, California ranked a lowly thirty-eighth among all states in fourth-grade math proficiency and thirty-sixth in eighth-grade math, as measured by National Assessment for Educational Progress (NAEP) exams.[84] Similarly, the California Science Test, developed by the California Department of Education to measure students' academic progress, found that, statewide, a mere 32 percent of fifth-graders, 31 percent of eighth-graders, and 28 percent of high school students met or exceeded the established standards for competency in science.[85] Also in recent years, violent crime in the state has skyrocketed[86] as Democrat politicians have pushed to defund the police, openly encouraged Antifa and BLM riots, and emptied state prisons of tens of thousands of convicted criminals.[87]

In 1970, California's population was 19.95 million people. In 2019, the most recent year for which comprehensive statistics are available, the state's population was 39.5 million—a 100 percent increase in half a century.

While the population doubled because of the massive influx of illegal immigrants, violent crime in California grew much faster. In 2019, the total number of violent crimes committed statewide was 364 percent higher than they were in 1970. The corresponding spikes in the incidence of specific offenses were as follows: 174 percent for murder, 418 percent for forcible rape, 242 percent for robbery, and 462 percent for aggravated assault.[88]

Now, after half a century of explosive growth, California's population has begun to decline. At least in part because of California's oppressive tax burden, residents have begun leaving the state in droves. In 2020, California's population declined by approximately 70,000 people—after having grown in every previous year, without exception, since 1900.[89]

Corporations, too, have fled the state in search of places with more hospitable business climates. According to the California Policy Center, at least fifty large corporations left California between 2014 and early 2021—with most of them departing in 2019 and 2020. Many of these companies, like Oracle, relocated to Republican-governed Texas, where tax and regulation policies are much more favorable to businesses. Some examples: First Foundation Bank moved its holding company to Dallas; Oracle, Hewlett Packard Enterprise, Tesla, QuestionPro, and ZP Better all relocated to Austin, as did Digital Realty Trust's enormous data center. Apple announced the construction of a new campus in Austin as well. Amazing Magnets moved its headquarters to Round Rock, a suburb of Austin. And SignEasy, Charles Schwab, and the $23 billion CBRE Group moved to Dallas.[90]

Culture matters. In their zeal to remake the world, Democrats have ignored the consequences of their actions and the human tragedies they have caused. Open borders is a terrible idea. No other country of consequence has them. In their zeal to gain political power, Democrats have grossly diminished the societies they govern and the lives in their care.

5

Reimagining the Law

W HEN BARACK OBAMA was elected the first black president in the nation's history, most Americans breathed a sigh of relief thinking they were entering a post-racial era where the greatest wound in the American soul would finally be healed. Raised by a white Marxist family, which his black father had abandoned, Obama won the presidency with 43 percent of the white vote, the largest share of any Democrat presidential candidate in a two-man race since Jimmy Carter in 1976.[1] Accordingly, Obama presented himself as the leader of the entire nation regardless of one's ethnicity, race, or even political affiliation. "We have never been a collection of red states and blue states," Obama famously said, "we are, and always will be, the United States." It was a popular, but deceptive line that Joe Biden would paraphrase during his presidential run.[2]

Probably no Americans at the time would have suspected that, far from entering an era in which race no longer mattered, they were instead entering a time when racial tensions and racial hatreds would reach levels not seen
since the passage of the Civil Rights Act of 1964. Few could
have imagined a scenario in which white Americans would
replace blacks as the targets of mindless bigotry because of
their skin color, and be subjected to open expressions of
racial hatred not seen since the days of the Ku Klux Klan.[3]

But unlike Ku Klux Klan racists, these virulent haters of white people were not representatives of backwa-
ter communities. They spoke instead from the editorial
rooms of *The New York Times, The Washington Post, The Atlantic,* the faculties of colleges and universities, and other
platforms of America's cultural elites. Dozens of courses
at America's top universities billed along the lines of
Whiteness Studies were dedicated to the proposition that
whiteness—the culture, habits and even character traits
of America's European-descended populations—are inherently evil and needed to be "abolished." A magazine
launched in 1992 by a Harvard graduate summed up in
its motto the new creed concerning white people: "Treason to Whiteness is Loyalty to Humanity."[4]

The Old Radicalism and the New

The very terms "white supremacy" and "white skin privilege," which the left has now embraced, were introduced
into the language of political discourse by the Weather
Underground terrorists who blew up police stations and

bombed the Pentagon in the 1970s. Like a deranged mirror image of the crazed cult figure Charles Manson, the Weather Underground saw themselves as the vanguard of an already-in-progress global race war between white oppressors and black freedom fighters. Their chosen role was to commit treason to whites by attacking "Amerikka" from within. In service to this cause, they had abetted the jail escape of Black Lives Matter's patron saint, convicted cop-killer Assata Shakur, enabling her flight to Cuba's communist dictatorship, which was their ideological motherland.

In an infamous incident in 1981, members of the Black Liberation Organization, along with veterans of the Weather Underground, who had joined forces with the "May 19th Communist Organization," robbed a Brink's armored truck in Nanuet, New York, killing a security guard and two policemen from nearby Nyack, one of whom was the first black hired by the Nyack police force. The murders left nine children fatherless.[5]

Among those convicted of the crime were former radicals Kathy Boudin and her husband David Gilbert. With the help of *The New York Times* editors who printed glowing stories of her alleged reformation in prison, where she wrote an article for the *Harvard Educational Review*, Boudin was paroled and released in 2003. There was no indication, however, that she had given up any of her radical views. While Boudin was in prison, she turned over her son Chesa to be raised by Weather Underground terrorists Bernardine Dohrn and Bill Ayers.[6] Even though Ayers admitted to participating in bombings of the New York

City Police Department headquarters, the U.S. Capitol building, and the Pentagon, and he and Dohrn were indicted for conspiracy to bomb police stations and government buildings, those charges were eventually dropped due to the prosecutorial misconduct of the FBI during its investigation of the group. Dohrn would later receive a $1,500 fine and three years' probation for her terrorist activities.[7]

In 2019, with the financial backing of George Soros, Chesa Boudin became the District Attorney of San Francisco. Operating under the same theories as his parents and step-parents, now shared by Democrat municipal office holders from Minneapolis to Portland, Boudin regarded black criminals as oppressed and simply refused to prosecute them. As in many cities with Soros-backed prosecutors—Philadelphia and St. Louis being two of the most notorious—Boudin's pro-criminal attitudes led to a crime wave.[8]

Boudin's stepfather, unrepentant Weather Underground member Bill Ayers, became an influential professor of education at the University of Illinois and a political ally of Barack Obama during his rise to power.[9]

With Obama's reelection in 2012, he took it on himself to become an enabler of the new Democrat Party anti-white racism. Rejecting his previous vision of a united America, he now said: "The legacy of slavery, Jim Crow, discrimination in almost every institution of our lives: You know, that casts a long shadow and that's still part of our DNA that's passed on. We're not cured of it."[10] In other words, Obama inaugurated the new politics of

Critical Race Theory: America is declared a bipolar nation of two colors, white oppressors and black victims, and its racism is so ingrained, so "systemic", it is a permanent feature of American life.

Putting actions behind those words, Obama made one of America's most prominent racial demagogues, Al Sharpton, his point man on civil rights. This was a man who incited the torching of a Harlem store because it was owned by a "white interloper"—as it happens, a Jew.[11] The arsonist was a supporter of Sharpton's National Action Network, and his deed resulted in the deaths of eight people of color who were in the store at the time, including himself.[12] At George Floyd's memorial, Floyd's family selected Sharpton to give the eulogy. Sharpton obliged with an openly racist speech in which he claimed that blacks were prevented from achieving their dreams because of an alleged "knee" that white America had pressed on their necks for 401 years.[13]

> George Floyd's story has been the story of black folks because ever since 401 years ago, the reason we could never be who we wanted and dreamed of being is you kept your knee on our neck. We were smarter than the underfunded schools you put us in, but you had your knee on our neck. We could run corporations and not hustle in the street, but you had your knee on our neck. We had creative skills, we could do whatever anybody else could do, but we couldn't get your knee off our neck. What happened to Floyd happens every day in this country, in education, in health services, and in every area of American life, it's time for us to

stand up in George's name and say "get your knee off our necks."[14]

Equally indicative of Obama's commitment to the new anti-white racism was the support he gave to the leaders of the Black Lives Matter organization, co-founded by a self-described trained Marxist and protégé of Weather Underground agitator Eric Mann. Obama's support consisted of multiple invitations to the White House for leading black activists during the deadly protests they had instigated. At these sessions, he praised them. "They are much better organizers than I was when I was at their age, and I am confident that they are going to take America to new heights," Obama said in February 2016.[15]

Disturbingly, one of Obama's invitations to the White House, and encouragement of Black Lives Matter, came just days after the assassination of five Dallas police officers by a deranged black racist named Micah Xavier Johnson in July 2016. Johnson, a BLM supporter, told a hostage negotiator that he had acted alone, was angry about the recent police shootings of two black men, and was determined to "kill white people—especially white police officers."[16] After several hours of negotiations, in which Johnson laughed, lied, and asked whether he had killed more police than had been reported, Dallas's black police chief concluded that further talk was futile and ordered his officers to blow up the still armed and threatening Johnson, using a remote-controlled robot.[17]

Disregarding the fact that the police chief who gave the order was black and the killer a homicidal maniac, the Marxist leader of Black Lives Matter, Patrisse Khan-Cullors, portrayed the incident as a case of white supremacists "lynching" yet another innocent black victim: "In the early morning hours of July 8, 2016, [Micah Johnson] became the first individual ever to be blown up by local law enforcement. They used a military-grade bomb against Micah Johnson and programmed a robot to deliver it to him. No jury, no trial."[18] Of course, Khan-Cullors' whole movement was in the business of convicting police officers of murder in advance of any jury or trial or investigation of the facts.

At a memorial service for the murdered officers, Obama took the opportunity to lecture the police survivors and the grieving families of the murdered police victims that white racism was ultimately responsible for what had happened, and that it was still part of America's DNA: "We also know that centuries of racial discrimination, of slavery, and subjugation, and Jim Crow; they didn't simply vanish with the law against segregation . . . we know that bias remains."[19]

Black Lives Matter

The Democrat Party had already enthusiastically endorsed Black Lives Matter and its many fictional slanders, despite or perhaps because of its leaders' dedication to convicted domestic terrorists such as cop-killer Assata Shakur. Biden campaign staffers even donated money to the Minnesota Freedom Fund, an organization that funded bail for the rioters charged with serious crimes.[20] Kamala Harris expressed her support of the cause, and Biden campaign staffers and other Democrat leaders contributed to it on the grounds that these violent criminals were peaceful protesters and thus martyrs for social justice.[21]

On the very day Joe Biden assumed the office of the presidency, he described the inspiration for one of his first Executive Orders as "a historic movement for justice [which] has highlighted the unbearable human costs of systemic racism," a clear allusion to Black Lives Matter.[22] A more accurate description of what Black Lives Matter had done was to highlight and exploit the lies of the new anti-white, anti-cop hatred that was driving the left's violent assaults on American cities.

One had only to look at the Democrats' exploitation of the death of George Floyd as a symbol of white inhumanity and racist oppression of expendable blacks. As it happens, Derek Chauvin, the officer whose knee was on George Floyd's neck, was married at the time to a "woman of color," and was assisted throughout Floyd's arrest by three other officers, two of whom were members of minority groups.[23]

There was no evidence that race played any role whatsoever in Officer Derek Chauvin's treatment of George Floyd or in Floyd's death. A prime witness to this almost universally overlooked fact was Minnesota's black Attorney General Keith Ellison. Ellison was a former Democrat National Committee deputy chair, and a current supporter of the violent terrorist group Antifa.[24] Previously he had spent eleven years as a spokesman for Louis Farrakhan's Nation of Islam.

As Attorney General, Ellison was in charge of the prosecution of Derek Chauvin in the George Floyd case. In an interview on CBS's *60 Minutes* after the verdict was delivered, Ellison said there was no evidence George Floyd was the victim of a hate crime or of racial bias. "I wouldn't call it that because hate crimes are crimes where there's an explicit motive and bias," Ellison said. "We don't have any evidence that Derek Chauvin factored in George Floyd's race as he did what he did." In other words, all the outrage against police racism, and all the mayhem fueled by that outrage because of the treatment of George Floyd, was based on no evidence whatsoever. It was based on a lie.

This rush to judgment in advance of the facts was not an anomaly for the national lynch mob that Black Lives Matter had assembled and inflamed over the eight years of its existence.[25] In every case around which Black Lives Matter mobilized its protests and riots, the verdict of "murder" was established at the very outset, in advance of the facts and the trial. Congresswoman Maxine Waters, now Chair of the House Financial Services Committee, even flew to Minnesota to demand a verdict of "Guilty, Guilty, Guilty."[26] This was the behavior of a lynch mob.

Yet Waters received no censure from her party or from any Democrat politician for this blatant attack on due process and the civil rights guaranteed under the U.S. Constitution. Indeed, Biden announced that he was "praying" for the right verdict—it's easy to deduce which verdict that might be.[27] Not only did this lynch mob mentality prevail in advance of investigations and trials, but in defiance of the facts they revealed. The Black Lives Matter narrative in which blacks were the racist prey of cops guilty of murder was set in stone no matter how absurd the claims were when confronted by the evidence.

The case of the drug dealer Freddie Gray in Baltimore was a clarifying instance of this abuse. Gray's death in custody triggered massive riots, accompanied by chants of "No Justice, No Peace, No Racist Police!" The rioters burned 144 vehicles and 15 buildings, injured 20 police officers, and required the National Guard and 5,000 officers from the mid-Atlantic region to re-establish civic order.[28]

Freddie Gray was a career criminal who had been arrested more than a dozen times in a seven-year period since he was 18. On April 12, 2015, he was arrested by Baltimore police, but violently resisted. He was placed in the back of a police van by several officers and taken unaccompanied to a local hospital to deal with injuries he might have suffered in the scuffle when he resisted arrest. When he arrived at the R Adams Cowley Shock Trauma Center at the University of Maryland, he was having trouble breathing. Seven days later he was dead.[29]

Six police officers were charged with his murder, three of them black. Four were acquitted and two had their cases dismissed. Speaking for the Black Lives Matter movement, Brittany Packnett, a frequent visitor to the Obama White House, declared: "In the wake of acquittal after acquittal, the message continues to be clear: not only do black lives, hearts and spines not matter to a system that continually kills us, but the only people who seem to be guilty of our deaths are ourselves."[30] It was one more outrageous lie.

Black political commentator and 2021 California gubernatorial candidate Larry Elder was so outraged by the absurdity of Packnett's anti-white propaganda that he posted a succinct response online:

FREDDIE GRAY DIED (2015)
POTUS: black
U.S. AG: black
Baltimore Mayor: black
City Council: mostly black
PD Head: black
Asst PD Head: black
St. Atty: black
3 of 6 cops charged. black
Judge who 2x ruled not guilty: black[31]

Critical Race Theory

The reckless lies of Black Lives Matter activists can only be understood in the context of their revolutionary outlook as trained Marxists. In the preceding years, Marxism had undergone a sea change, focusing on cultural and racial oppressions along with its traditional economic ones. In its new form as Critical Race Theory, Marxism shaped the ideological prejudices of all components of the radical left, and more recently the radical leadership of the

Consequences

The anti-police propaganda spread by Black Lives Matter during the near decade of its existence has had a traumatic impact on law enforcement and the communities they protect. Indictments of officers for crimes they didn't commit have provided the rationale for "stand down" orders by local governments in the face of the violent riots to protest George Floyd's death. In Minneapolis–St. Paul, Portland, Seattle, and eventually hundreds of locations, police were ordered by Democrat politicians to stand down while rioters tore their cities apart, set entire city blocks on fire, and destroyed businesses, court houses, and police departments. In Democrat-run cities across the country, left-wing mayors and district attorneys held the police back while looters and thugs turned vast swaths of their municipalities into war zones.[36]

Most of those who took part in the mayhem were immunized from incarceration by the same authorities. This was partly because of the no-bail laws that Democrats had passed. As the *New York Post* reported: "Right now, anyone arrested for looting gets rapidly released, with no need to post bail to avoid jail until trial. . . ."[37] Even more support was provided to the street criminals by national leaders of the Democrat Party. Senator and soon-to-be-Vice President Kamala Harris publicly announced her support for the Minnesota Freedom Fund, an organization that made bail payments on behalf of people who were arrested for crimes committed during the Minneapolis riots and were awaiting trial. Thanks in part to Harris's endorsement, the Minnesota Freedom Fund received more than $35 million in donations.[38] At least 13 staff members of Joe Biden's presidential campaign made personal donations to the Fund as well.[39]

At the same time, officials were releasing tens of thousands of criminals from prison, using Covid-19 as a transparent excuse. Prosecutors funded by the radical billionaire George Soros were openly decriminalizing crime as well. In San Francisco, radical district attorney Chesa Boudin announced that he would not enforce laws against so-called "quality of life" crimes such as public urination, prostitution, and drug use.[40] He also asserted that the bail system is unjust because it "allows the wealthy to purchase their freedom" while "the poor languish behind bars even when they pose no risk and the evidence against them is weak."[41] These pro-criminal agendas (always justified as defenses of the oppressed) were the inevitable result of the Democrats' crusade against "systemic racism," with its presumption that disproportionate numbers of blacks in prison were not responsible for their acts but were victims of white supremacy and systemic racism.

Inevitably, looting by blacks was regarded by Black Lives Matter and other radical groups as "reparations for slavery." As one BLM organizer, Ariel Atkins, preposterously said in the aftermath of an August 2020 riot: "I don't care if someone decides to loot a Gucci or a Macy's or a Nike store, because that makes sure that person eats. That makes sure that person has clothes. That is reparations. Anything they wanted to take, they can take it because these businesses have insurance."[42] In a similar spirit, a social media post for an August 2020 BLM rally encouraged activists to come out and support looters who had been arrested for "taking reparations from corporations."[43]

When the Covid-19 pandemic began to recede in the fall of 2020, the excuse for releasing convicted felons became prison overcrowding. In April 2021, it was reported that beginning on May 1 California would allow 76,000 inmates to be released before their sentences ran out. This included more than 63,000 inmates convicted of violent crimes, nearly 20,000 of whom were serving life sentences who could now use good-behavior credits to shorten their sentences by as much as one-third, instead of the existing maximum reduction of one-fifth. Thirteen thousand of the inmates were in prison for serious but nonviolent offenses and would be eligible for early release after serving just half their sentences.[44]

Releasing criminals, ordering police to stand down in the midst of insurrectionary violence, failing to arrest rioters, raising tax-exempt funds to provide their bail when they were arrested, passing "no cash bail" ordinances that set them free as soon as they were arrested, declaring thefts misdemeanors, were all agendas implemented by radical—and racist—Democrat mayors, prosecutors, and city councils in major urban centers like Minneapolis, New York, Portland, Seattle, St. Louis, Atlanta, and Washington, D.C.

The effect on law enforcement was catastrophic. Within a month of George Floyd's death, the New York Police chief, Terence Monahan, was already in shock over the disrespect government officials and civilians alike were showing for law enforcement, declaring that "the animosity towards police has been absolutely unbelievable."[45] In Milwaukee that same month, homicides were up 100 percent, a statistic about which Milwaukee Inspector Terrence Gordon commented: "Morale [among police] is terrible. . . . It's because they're afraid that nobody in this community is going to stand up for them. In twenty-five years, I've never seen it like this. I never thought that I'd see the day where a Milwaukee police officer would withdraw from the community they swore to serve. But I can see it beginning to happen right now, and it's just terrible, because on the other side of all these crimes are victims."[46]

Defund the Police

In Minneapolis, one month after George Floyd's death, the city council, all but one of whose thirteen members belong to the state's Democratic-Farmer-Labor party (the sole minority is a Green) voted unanimously to dismantle and abolish the city's police department and to "re-imagine" public safety by hiring social workers and therapists to replace them.[47] A month later, nearly 200 officers, amounting to one-fifth of the Minneapolis police force, had already filed paperwork to leave their jobs, citing post-traumatic stress. "It's almost like a nuclear bomb hit the city, and the people who didn't perish are standing around," said veteran officer Rich Walker Sr. "I'm still surprised that we've got cops showing up to work, to be honest."[48]

On June 16, 2021, the fifty-odd officers who made up Portland's Rapid Response Team voted to disband their unit after one member, Officer Corey Budworth, was indicted on a fourth-degree assault charge stemming from a baton strike against a rioter ten months earlier. "Have I ever seen anything like this in my career? No, I don't think any of us have," said Deputy Chief Chris Davis regarding the lack of support that the Rapid Response Team was receiving from City Hall.[49]

Within weeks of Floyd's death, Black Lives Matter launched a "Defund the Police" campaign. Democrats on New York's city council responded by cutting its police budget by $1 billion and announcing that it would permanently disband the department's elite Anti-Crime Unit. The unit was comprised of 600 undercover plainclothes officers who targeted illegal guns and local crime sprees.[50] Similar budget and personnel cuts were announced in nearly two dozen additional Democrat-controlled cities including Chicago, Los Angeles, San Francisco, Seattle, and Portland.[51]

During a June 30, 2020, appearance on MSNBC's *Morning Joe*, New York mayor (and Castro enthusiast) Bill de Blasio hailed the "profound change" that would be taking place in New York because of the defunding of the police, declaring against all odds that it would mean the creation of a "safer city in the future." He announced that he would take some of the money cut from the police budget and use it to fund the painting of the words "Black Lives Matter," in massive yellow letters, on the pavement of Fifth Avenue, "right in front of Trump Tower," he said.

"We're going to take this moment in history and amplify it by taking the 'Black Lives Matter' symbolism and putting it all over this city."[52]

It was entirely political. None of the reform measures were based on evidence of police misconduct or systemic racism. They were products of the hysteria Black Lives Matter and its leftist allies had whipped up over George Floyd's death and the alleged martyrdoms of innocent blacks murdered for their skin color. In reality, the principal victims of the crime wave that Democrats' attacks on police created were inner-city blacks who relied on them as their first and only real line of defense.

The hypocrisy of the Democrats and their radical war against the system was dramatically displayed by "Squad" member Cori Bush. Bush was a leading and impassioned advocate of defunding the police and replacing them with mental health experts. In July 2021 it was revealed that Bush had spent $70,000 in campaign funds for a private security force to protect her over a three-month period. Evidently, law enforcement was not the problem, except for those who guarded ordinary people and the poor.[53]

Rising Carnage in the Inner Cities

Far from laying the groundwork for safer cities, the attacks on police led to dramatic increases in violent crime rates across the nation. In a study of 57 U.S. cities, New Orleans–based data consultant Jeff Asher found that total homicides had risen in 51 of those 57 cities during

2020, and that the average increase in homicides was 36.7 percent. In cities that were the targets of Black Lives Matter riots, the upsurge in homicides was dramatically worse. Homicides were up 72.3 percent in Minneapolis, 74.1 percent in Seattle, and 78.2 percent in Louisville.[54]

According to Manhattan Institute scholar Heather MacDonald, "the rising carnage in the inner city is the consequence of [the] official repudiation of the criminal-justice system. The current tolerance and justification for vandalism and violence; the silencing of police supporters; and police unwillingness to intervene, even when their own precincts are assaulted—all send a clear message to criminals that society has lost the will to prevent lawlessness."[55]

Not so for Democrats. In regard to violent crime, they refused to confront the responsibility of individuals for their actions, focusing instead on what they call "gun violence," as though guns and not individuals perpetrate the crimes. The reason for this myopia is their commitment to a radical ideology that is pursuing a race war against a society it has labeled as white supremacist. Advancing this war requires them to ignore the individuals who commit the crimes and their motivations for doing so.

To focus on the criminals rather than their instruments, Democrats would have to confront the fact that while black males make up 6 percent of the population, they commit half the nation's murders and robberies and more than 36 percent of all violent crimes.[56] Blacks also account for more than 80 percent of the victims of those crimes.[57] For radicals, these facts complicate and compromise the war they are waging against allegedly racist police forces whose innocent targets are black. Therefore, they are wholly silent about the epidemic of black-on-black crime and its prevalence in the urban centers they control.

By August 2020, the criminal takeover of the streets that had resulted in shootings, lootings, car jackings, and physical assaults had created a public backlash so great that Democrats were growing uneasy about its impact on the 2022 midterm elections. Thinking he would trap the Democrats into recording their support for the mayhem resulting from their Defund the Police efforts, Republican Senator Tommy Tuberville proposed an amendment to a spending bill that would withdraw federal funding from cities that supported the Defund movement. However, the amendment's language was nonbinding and thus amounted to nothing more than a suggestion.

Led by Senator Cory Booker, the Democrats pounced on Tuberville's amendment as a gift that would allow them to seem supportive of the police, while at the same time they could tell their radical base that in practice it amounted to nothing. On August 10 the Senate voted 99-0 to pass the Tuberville amendment. An ecstatic Booker crowed: "I am sure I will see no [Republican] political ads attacking anybody here over defund the police." Booker then urged his Democrat colleagues "not to walk but to sashay" into the House chamber to cast their votes in support of Tuberville's amendment.[58]

Criminal Guns

Fast forward to a few months into Joe Biden's presidency: Outrage over the spiking crime rates continued to soar, forcing Joe Biden to address the subject in a major speech from the White House. On June 23, 2021, Biden told Americans that the villains behind the explosion of violent crime were legal gun dealers. The remedy, he said, was a "zero-tolerance policy" for gun dealers should they break existing federal laws. A White House official explained that the zero-tolerance policy for gun dealers meant that, "absent extraordinary circumstances that would need to be justified to the director, ATF will seek to revoke the licenses of dealers that first time that they violate federal law." The White House then assured the public: "This will be a historic policy that will make sure that we hold gun dealers across the country who are contributing to the supply of crime guns accountable."[59] As usual, no evidence was provided by Biden or his staff that guns illegally bought from licensed gun dealers played any role in the homicides committed during the crime wave.

One effect of the Democrats' radical view of the problem was to mistake their policy of blaming the police as a view shared by the black community itself. In fact, the opposite was true. A Gallup poll taken in August 2020 revealed that 81 percent of black respondents said that they wanted the police presence in their neighborhoods to either remain the same or increase.[60] As Reason.com noted: "Ironically, the new survey on feelings toward law enforcement presence ... suggests that if Black Lives Matters and other police abolitionists get their way, they will be thwarting the views of the very group in whose name they are acting."

Nearly a year later, as the crime epidemic continued to spread with murders in broad daylight in the nation's capital and victims including a 6-year-old girl, one black police chief had enough. "I'm mad as hell," D.C. police chief Robert Contee told a crowd. "Enough is enough. We want to help people, but you cannot coddle violent criminals. You cannot. You cannot treat violent criminals who are out here making communities unsafe for you, your loved ones.... They might not want a job. They might not need services. What they may require is to be off of our streets because they're making it unsafe for us.... If not, then we see more of this."[61]

6

Corona Control

FROM THE MOMENT the coronavirus reached America, the
Democrat Party deployed it as a weapon against Donald
Trump and the Republicans. When Trump banned travel
from China on January 31, 2020, Democrats including Joe
Biden and Nancy Pelosi were downplaying the seriousness
of the pandemic. They denounced Trump as a racist and xenophobe.[1]

When there was a shortage of masks and ventilators,
Democrats blamed Trump, although it turned out that
the shortages were caused by the Obama administration's
failure to restock the supplies after they were depleted
during the Ebola epidemic.[2] In short order, working with
private companies, Trump produced ventilators in record
numbers.

When China's dark role in concealing the dangers of the virus was revealed and Trump began referring to Covid-19 as the China Virus, the Democrats called him a racist and were applauded by the Chinese communists for doing so.[3]

When the 2020 presidential campaign got into high gear, one of Biden's main themes was that Trump had bungled the government's response to the epidemic. "We're more than eight months into this crisis," Biden told an audience in October, "and the president still doesn't have a plan."[4]

In fact, Trump did have a plan. He called it Operation Warp Speed, his administration's $20 billion initiative to work with pharmaceutical companies to develop and mass-produce a safe and effective Covid-19 vaccine by the end of the year. Democrats were skeptical—that it could either be done or that such a fast-tracked vaccine would be safe. Biden and his running mate, Kamala Harris, even expressed reservations about whether "Trump's vaccine" should be taken at all.[5] Vice President Harris went so far as to say she wouldn't take it "if Trump tells me to."[6]

Despite the odds, Trump's ambitious initiative worked. On December 11, 2020, about a year after the world first heard about the Covid-19 virus, the Food and Drug administration approved for emergency use a new type of vaccine, known as a messenger or mRNA vaccine, produced by Pfizer. It approved Moderna's similar vaccine a week later. By the time Biden took office, 30 million doses of the Covid vaccines had already been administered.[7]

Although this proved a turning point in the epidemic and provided a powerful stimulus to the economic recovery, the Democrats did not pause long enough in their Trump hatred to give Trump credit. Biden even attempted to take credit himself, just as throughout his career he'd taken credit for speeches and articles plagiarized from other politicians.[8] "Two months ago, this country didn't have nearly enough vaccine supply to vaccinate all or anywhere near all of the American public, but soon we will," Biden stated during his first national address as president. "Now, because of all the work we've done, we'll have enough vaccine supply for all adults in America by the end of May. That's months ahead of schedule."[9] But it was not the work he and his associates had done; it was the work that the much maligned Donald Trump had done that had turned the Covid-19 tide.

"There's no reason to be walking around with a mask"

From the outset, the Democrats' response to the pandemic was marked by confusing, often contradictory messages. At first, the Democrats and health officials such as Dr. Anthony Fauci, Director of the National Institute of Allergy and Infectious Diseases (NIAID), said that the use of face masks in public was unnecessary—the official position at the time of both the Chinese-controlled World Health Organization and the Centers for Disease Control and Prevention.

"There's no reason to be walking around with a mask," Fauci told *60 Minutes* on March 8, 2020. While masks may block some droplets, he said, they do not provide the level of protection people think they do.[10] "When you're in the middle of an outbreak," Fauci went on, "wearing a mask might make people feel a little bit better and it might even block a droplet, but it's not providing the perfect protection that people think that it is. And often, there are unintended consequences—people keep fiddling with the mask and they keep touching their face."

Within weeks, both Fauci and the Democrats did a complete about-face, declaring that mask wearing was now not only essential but also a patriotic duty. Joe Biden made mask-wearing into a kind of fetish, never being seen without one. He announced that, were he elected president, he would make wearing a mask in public mandatory nationwide. "I would do everything possible to make it required that people had to wear masks in public," he said.[11] The politics of this new posture were evident. In an effort to encourage public optimism and reopen the businesses that were being shut down, mainly by Democrat governors, Trump had made it a practice to always appear in public not wearing a mask.

The science hadn't changed to justify the Biden mask mandates, which raised serious questions about government policies and individual freedom. One study in the *New England Journal of Medicine* declared, "Wearing a mask outside health care facilities offers little, if any, protection from infection," and "[t]he chance of catching Covid-19 from a passing interaction in a public space is therefore minimal."[12] In issuing his mandates, Biden ignored the science.

What had changed was the politics. The Democrats now saw that by ordering every man, woman, and child in the country to wear face masks, they could blame Trump and his advisers for not wearing masks and being derelict in the battle against the virus. At the same time, forcing people to wear masks was a test of power, asserting the government's authority to act by fiat and compel the public to obey its commands.

Fifteen Days to Flatten the Curve

Between mid-February and mid-March 2020, as Trump's last year in office began, the stock market went into free fall. The Dow lost 37 percent of its value in 30 days, plummeting from a record high of 29,551 on February 12 to 18,591 on March 23.[13] It was the worst market drop since the 2008–2009 crash.

Democrat leaders took note. They saw blood in the water—and a huge opportunity. The economy was Trump's strongest selling point. What if the Covid pandemic threatened all of that?

Within days, Democrats began pushing for an unprecedented shutdown of the entire economy. Because of the escalating spread of the virus, the Trump administration put off its attempt to reopen the economy and recommended that the public continue to avoid mass gatherings and maintain social distance from others through April 30.[14] Believing that the viral threat was greater than pushing the country into an economic depression, Democrat mayors and governors began ordering "nonessential" businesses to be closed by executive orders. Public schools were shuttered, religious services cancelled, and medical treatments not related to Covid were denied. People out on the street without a good excuse were fined, in some cases even arrested.[15] It was almost *de facto* martial law that was achieved in Democrat-run states like California and Michigan and New York.

When accusations of opportunism were directed at the Democrats, their defense was that they were only following the science. As for the lockdowns, stay-at-home orders, and public school closures, these would only be temporary, Democrat governors assured the public. All the country needed was "fifteen days to flatten the curve," beginning in mid-March 2020, to prevent hospitals and health care facilities from being flooded with dying Covid patients.[16]

Censoring "Misinformation"

Of course, not everyone agreed with the Democrats' dire assessment of a future without draconian measures to control the virus's spread. To mute their critics, Democrats attempted to ban "misinformation" from social media outlets and the news. House Speaker Nancy Pelosi called on the media and Big Tech to remove news articles, opinion columns, scientific papers, and even entire books that contradicted the official position of the CDC and Dr. Anthony Fauci, a lifetime Democrat.[17]

This political strategy remained in place after Biden's victory in the November election. Any dissent, even by highly qualified PhDs and medical doctors, was deemed "misinformation" that, the new president said, was "killing people."[18]

A Cornucopia of Unpaid-For Relief

While Trump was promising hope in terms of reopening the economy and generating new wealth, the congressional Democrats promised an unprecedented flood of borrowed government money to ease the pain. The money would come from the sale of U.S. Treasury bonds to the nation's banks.[19] Republicans, not wanting to be left out, agreed to both the 15-day nationwide shutdown to flatten the curve beginning March 15 and to the Coronavirus Aid, Relief, and Economic Security (CARES) Act, which included $300 billion in direct payments to Americans, $367 billion in Small Business Administration loans, and $500 billion in loans to big corporations and local governments.[20]

Their relief bill included approximately $2.2 trillion in direct cash payments, salary guarantees, mortgage forbearance orders, and extended unemployment benefits.[21] It was the largest expansion of government programs since the New Deal, and overnight tens of millions of Americans found themselves the beneficiaries of direct government payouts.[22]

The bipartisan legislation passed the Senate unanimously and was signed by Trump on March 27, 2020. Later, the government pushed to increase the spending to a staggering $6 trillion, including the Families First

Coronavirus Response Act (March 2020), the Paycheck Protection Program and Health Care Enhancement Act (April 2020), and the infrastructure bill.[23]

The predicted surge in Covid hospitalizations never materialized, however. Instead, the public, stuck at home and unemployed, watched TikTok videos of nurses doing dance routines in nearly empty hospitals.[24] The "15 days to flatten the curve" turned into more than a year as the pandemic in the United States peaked not in mid-2020, when the experts predicted it would, but in early 2022.[25] Along the way, the decrees from Democrat politicians grew increasingly authoritarian as Covid gradually spread from state to state.

In Democrat-controlled states such as California, New York, Michigan, and Illinois, governors and mayors issued unprecedented and, as was later determined, unconstitutional orders banning all public assemblies, political protests, and religious services (except for Democrat approved groups such as Black Lives Matter).[26]

Not the Science

By the time Joe Biden took office in January 2021, it was becoming increasingly clear that the lockdowns the Democrats had pushed for had successfully destroyed the booming Trump economy but had little impact on the pandemic, which was about to slow dramatically as a result of the new vaccines. California, for example, had instituted the strictest lockdowns in the country, yet it had twice the number of cases per capita compared to states such as Florida, which locked down only briefly or not at all.[27]

In fact, by July 2021 the states with the highest overall death rates per capita from Covid—New Jersey (242 deaths per 100,000 people), New York (223), and Massachusetts (211)—were all Democrat strongholds and had the most stringent lockdown policies.[28] At the same time, many of the states that either quickly lifted lockdown orders and mask mandates or never imposed them at all saw far fewer Covid casualties: Florida (123), Texas (126), Georgia (118), and Idaho (96).[29]

This meant that it was possible to battle Covid-19 effectively without destroying the livelihoods of tens of millions of citizens and forcing children to remain locked at home, away from in-person schooling.

Did the U.S. Government Fund Chinese Virus Research?

Early in the pandemic, Donald Trump insisted that he was confident, based on intelligence evidence he had seen, that the coronavirus originated in a Chinese government virology lab in Wuhan.[30] Trump's suggestion was immediately and vociferously condemned by both the corporate media and Democrat politicians as a racist "conspiracy theory."[31]

In fact, a task force of twenty-seven virology experts organized by Dr. Peter Daszak, the president of the U.S.-based nongovernmental organization EcoHealth Alliance and affiliated with the British medical journal *The*

Lancet, prepared a statement that specifically condemned the theory that the coronavirus originated in a Chinese or any laboratory.

"We stand together to strongly condemn conspiracy theories suggesting that Covid-19 does not have a natural origin," the scientists wrote.[32]

Later, Dr. Anthony Fauci, in testimony under oath before Congress, repeatedly referred to this statement from the group led by Daszak in his own rebuttal of the Chinese lab theory of the coronavirus's origins.

Yet by early 2021, new evidence had emerged that forced even many skeptical scientists to reconsider[33]—and news organizations to retract their characterizations of the lab-leak theory as patently false.[34]

"The possibility of a laboratory accident or inadvertent leak having caused the coronavirus outbreak must not be ignored," *The Washington Post* conceded in January, citing new information about Chinese government research into bat coronaviruses.[35] *The Wall Street Journal* reported that secret intelligence revealed that in November 2019, three researchers from the Wuhan Institute of Virology became suddenly so sick they were hospitalized.[36]

What's more, as Republican politicians began looking further into the origins of the Covid-19 pandemic, they discovered troubling links between Dr. Fauci's NIAID, Dr. Daszak's EcoHealth Alliance, and China's Wuhan Institute of Virology.

Dr. Fauci was called to testify throughout 2021 before Congressional committees, and, under direct questioning by senators, especially Sen. Rand Paul of Kentucky, he repeatedly denied that his institute had funded controversial "gain of function" research at the Chinese facility in Wuhan.

Gain of function research refers to attempts by scientists to take a deadly natural virus and genetically alter it in the laboratory so that it becomes transmissible to humans—ostensibly so that scientists can understand and prevent such a development in the future. Obviously, such research is a double-edged sword. It could also easily mutate into biological warfare research—since such artificially enhanced viruses could be used as bioweapons.

As a result, in 2014 the U.S. National Institutes of Health issued a ban on gain of function research but then rescinded its ban in October 2017, insisting that new research will be subject to "strict scrutiny" and face a "rigorous process."[37]

In a series of Senate hearings, Sen. Paul repeatedly asked Fauci if his organization, or any intermediary organization, had funded gain of function experiments in Wuhan. Fauci categorically insisted that it had not. His agency "has not ever and does not now fund gain of function research in the Wuhan Institute of Virology," Fauci declared under oath on May 1.[38]

But Paul refused to back down. "Dr. Fauci, knowing it is a crime to lie to Congress, do you wish to retract your statement?" the senator asked in a tense hearing in July 2021.

"I have never lied to Congress, and I do not retract that statement," Fauci replied angrily, adding that Paul, who is himself a medical doctor, didn't know what he was talking about.

"I totally resent the lie you are now propagating, Senator," he said.

Paul replied that gain of function research had been taking place in the Wuhan lab and that the NIH funded it, either directly or through intermediaries. "You can't get away from it," Paul said. "It meets your definition and you are obfuscating the truth."

In September 2021, the independent news organization *The Intercept* reported on a trove of 900 internal NIH documents that it had obtained under a Freedom of Information Act (FOIA) request that at least raised questions about the veracity of Fauci's earlier statements under oath.[39]

Included in the documents was a grant proposal filed with the Facui-led NIAID for research by EcoHealth Alliance, led by Dr. Daszak, into "Understanding the Risk of Bat Coronavirus Emergence."[40]

The $600,000 grant was for research in Wuhan that "will examine the risk of future coronavirus (CoV) emergence from wildlife using in-depth field investigations across the human-wildlife interface in China, molecular characterization of novel CoVs and host receptor binding domain genes, mathematical models of transmission and evolution, and in vitro and in vivo laboratory studies of host range."[41]

What did that mean in practice?

According to the *Washington Post*'s analysis, the Wuhan "researchers used reverse genetics to deliberately create novel recombinants of wild bat coronavirus backbones and spike genes, then tested the ability of these chimeric (man-made) viruses to replicate in—not just infect—a variety of cell lines."

The Chinese researchers discovered "novel coronavirus backbone and spike combinations that do not exist in nature and are capable of replicating efficiently in human cells with the angiotensin-converting enzyme 2 (ACE2), the protein that provides the entry point for the coronavirus to hook into and infect human tissue."[42]

In his testimony under oath, Fauci had claimed both that the NIH had not funded gain of function research in China—and that, either way, making bat virus transmissible to humans was not gain of function research anyway.[43] Paul and other critics insisted Fauci was playing legalistic word games, crafting a definition of "gain of function" in such a way that it excluded the very research his organization had funded.

Other virology experts agreed. Dr. Richard Ebright, a biosafety expert and a professor of chemistry and chemical biology at Rutgers University, told reporters that the Wuhan research "epitomizes" the definition of gain of function research since it involved working with pathogens "resulting from the enhancement of the transmissibility and/or virulence of a pathogen."[44]

In fact, Ebright said, the "documents make it clear that assertions by the NIH Director, Francis Collins, and the NIAID Director, Anthony Fauci, that the NIH did not support gain of function research or potential pandemic pathogen enhancement at WIV are untruthful."[45]

Even more troubling were emails, obtained under separate FOIA requests, that showed Fauci and other U.S.

virologists increasingly worried about public awareness that the coronavirus may have come from a Chinese lab.

Many of the 3,000 pages of emails are heavily redacted by government censors, but the visible portions of the documents reveal that U.S. researchers were worried that their work with Chinese laboratories might be viewed negatively by the public.

On April 16, 2020, Dr. Francis Collins, director of the National Institutes of Health, sent an email to Fauci and other U.S. health officials with the subject line "Conspiracy gains momentum." The obtained copy of the email included a link to a Mediaite report about a discussion on Fox News' *Hannity*, but the entire contents of the email itself were blacked out.

Yet two days later, Fauci received an email from Dr. Peter Daszak, the head of EcoHealth Alliance, which had subcontracted the research in Wuhan into "novel coronavirus backbone and spike combinations that do not exist in nature," thanking him for his help debunking the lab leak theory of Covid-19.

"I just wanted to say a personal thank you on behalf of our staff and collaborators for publicly standing up and stating that the scientific evidence supports a natural origin for Covid-19 from a bat-to-human spillover, not a lab release from the Wuhan Institute of Virology," Daszak wrote on April 18, 2020.[46]

Critics, including Rand Paul and others, allege that these revelations show that Fauci, Daszak, and other U.S. researchers had an obvious conflict of interest when it came to investigating the origins of the Covid-19 virus.[47]

If the Covid-19 pandemic was triggered by a viral release from a Chinese lab—whether or not the virus had been artificially enhanced to be transmissible to humans—it would not look very good if the U.S. government had provided even minimal funding to that lab.

Fauci and other virology experts now play a substantial role in dictating how billions of people across the planet live—which freedoms they maintain, which freedoms they are forced to surrender. If it turns out that the lab leak theory is correct, then some of these same experts could have played a small, indirect, certainly unintentional but quite real role in unleashing one of the deadliest pandemics in history.

Demonizing the Unvaxxed

When politics takes command, policies can become increasingly detached from reality. It didn't take long for the Democrats to go from being openly skeptical of "Trump's vaccine" to being vaccine hawks, insisting that it was a patriotic duty for every American to be vaccinated. Indeed, one of the odd ways in which Congressional Democrats, the Biden administration, and their many supporters in the media and Intelligence agencies responded to the Covid-19 pandemic was through the demonization of the so-called "unvaxxed."

This was odd because the Democrats had gone out of their way before the election to sympathize with those who felt that any Covid-19 vaccine developed in such a hurried way might not be safe, that the government might cut corners in order to demonstrate it was doing something about the pandemic. Despite this history, the Democrats quickly began to insult, belittle and then openly threaten anyone who hesitated to be vaccinated, even if they had legitimate health reasons (such as a history of allergic reactions to vaccines) to postpone vaccination. As usual, the Democrats put a racial twist on the issue, trying to find correlations between the "deplorables" (white Trump supporters) and "vaccine hesitancy." In fact, however, polls showed that the group most openly skeptical of the Covid-19 vaccine was black Americans, not whites.

Incredibly, in other words, national Democrats had gone out of their way to insult the very people they were trying to convince, insisting without evidence that the unvaccinated (many of whom had natural immunity from having caught the virus early in the pandemic) were the cause of the continuing pandemic. "If you're not vaccinated, you're not nearly as smart as I thought you were," Biden told reporters in July 2021. "Only one thing we know for sure, if those other 100 million people got vaccinated, we'd be in a very different world."[48]

Other Democrats joined the chorus. In August 2021, Arne Duncan, who served as Secretary of Education under former President Obama, took to Twitter to condemn the many Americans who opposed vaccine mandates for all. He likened such people to the ISIS-affiliated terrorist who, a few days earlier, had carried out a suicide bombing at Hamid Karzai International Airport in Kabul, killing thirteen American servicemen and more than 160 Afghan civilians. "Have you noticed how strikingly similar both the mindsets and actions between the suicide bombers at Kabul's airport and the anti-mask and anti-vax people here?" Duncan wrote on Twitter. "They both blow themselves up, inflict harm on those around them, and are convinced they are fighting for freedom."[49]

California Governor Gavin Newsom, fighting for his political life in a recall election over the hypocritical way he handled the pandemic, insisted that the unvaccinated were "murderous" and likened them to drunk drivers.[50] House Speaker Nancy Pelosi called unvaccinated members of Congress, such as Covid survivor Sen. Rand Paul, "selfish" and a danger to their colleagues.

The problem with this argument was that it undercut the premise that Covid vaccines are truly effective, since unvaccinated people would be a "threat" to the vaccinated only if the vaccines were not, as claimed, "98 percent effective."[51] Eventually the Democrats gave up entirely on persuasion and resorted to force. They encouraged industries from the airlines to restaurants to simply ban the unvaccinated, a strategy that legal analysts called "government by surrogate," since it allows the Democrats to avoid court challenges they would likely lose.

In May 2021, the Biden administration announced a new goal to administer at least one dose of Covid-19 vaccine to 70 percent of adults—and to have 160 million people fully vaccinated in the United States—by July 4. If Americans complied, Biden said, they might be able to have a few friends over to the house to celebrate the Fourth of July. "If we do all this, if we do our part, if we do this together, by July the 4th, there's a good chance you, your families, and friends will be able to get together in your backyard or in your neighborhood and have a cookout and a barbeque and celebrate Independence Day."[52]

This seemed utterly detached from reality, at the time. Americans could look at the case and death charts printed in most newspapers and online and see for themselves that the COVID-19 pandemic had peaked in the United States five months earlier, in late January 2021.[53]

As a candidate and then as president, Biden had promised that Americans would not be forced to take the vaccine if they didn't think it was necessary.[54] Biden himself had expressed sympathy for those skeptical of a Covid vaccine developed by the Trump administration.[55] But very soon, Democrats, businesses, and organizations across the country insisted that vaccination would be a requirement for everything from air travel to shopping for groceries.

"You've got to start telling people, if you don't get vaccinated, you can't come into this office or this place of business," explained CNN anchor Don Lemon, an unofficial spokesperson for the Democratic Party. "If you don't get vaccinated, you can't come to work. If you don't get vaccinated, you can't come into this gym. If you don't get vaccinated, you can't get onto this airplane. It has nothing to do with freedom. It has nothing to do with liberty."[56] But quite obviously, it was the greatest lockdown of all, allowing the government to curtail the freedom of every American at will.

In late July, Biden announced that vaccination or weekly testing would be required for all federal workers and members of the armed forces.[57] The scientific rationale provided for these draconian measures was the claim that mutations of the coronavirus, specifically the Delta variant, had created another dangerous situation that required drastic steps. The Delta variant was more contagious, they said, and seemed more harmful to younger people.

This claim was initially based on a study conducted in India, and rejected for peer-review, that focused on a vaccine not authorized for use in the United States.[58] However, the study was used by Biden and the CDC to make claims that people vaccinated against Covid-19 were just as likely as unvaccinated people to spread the virus's Delta variant.[59] While studies showed that vaccinated people could theoretically catch the Delta Variant—so-called "breakthrough infections" that can be, in some cases, transmissible—the actual numbers of cases in which this occurred was extremely small. According to the CDC's own data, of the 168 million people vaccinated in the United States only 8,054 people were hospitalized with a subsequent breakthrough infection—a "reinfection rate" of only 0.004 percent.[60]

Yet despite this, there were signs that Biden and his fellow Democrats had no intention of keeping their side of the bargain even if all Americans complied. The CDC recommended that even vaccinated people should wear face masks again in certain areas, and that all children in school should do so as well.[61] Even more inexplicably, the White House maintained that Americans could still be subject to future lockdowns—if that was the guidance from alleged experts.[62] It began to look as though the

Democrats were determined to make face masks, social distancing, on-again, off-again lockdowns, and dictatorial government orders permanent features of American life.

Internal Passports and State Control

Overnight, it seemed, America had been transformed from a nation of inalienable rights guaranteed by the Constitution—the right to assemble, to worship, to speak freely—into a nation in which those rights were now contingent upon doing what unelected health experts and government officials demanded.

Going to church, traveling, gathering together with family members, even sending children to school now would all require explicit permission from the government. It was reminiscent of a slogan that appeared in Berkeley, California, in the 1960s, at the height of that city's zany radicalism: *Everything not expressly permitted is forbidden.*

This fundamental transformation was encapsulated in the Democrats' push for "vaccine passports," which would contain an individual's vaccination and health records as a requirement for access to travel, entertainment venues, and whatever else the government decided.[63] It was a totalitarian restriction of individual freedom already pioneered in Communist China's "social credit" system.[64]

On August 3, 2021, New York City Mayor Bill de Blasio announced that a new vaccine passport, which he called the Key to NYC Pass,[65] would be required to enjoy most activities within the city limits, from visiting restaurants to grocery shopping. "We know that strong, clear mandates help," de Blasio declared in a press conference.[66] The mayor also said: "The Key to NYC: When you hear those words, I want you to imagine the notion that because someone is vaccinated they can do all the amazing things available in New York City. . . . If you are vaccinated, all that is going to open up to you, you have the key, you can open the door. If you are unvaccinated, unfortunately, you will not be able to participate in many things."[67]

This was so alien to the American idea, and the freedom that it promised, that it was difficult to understand how an American official could propose and institute it so cheerfully, although de Blasio's affection for Cuba's sadistic dictator Fidel Castro went a long way toward explaining his attitude.

As in the "democratic people's republics" in Eastern Europe under Communism, Americans were now being told that they would need the equivalent of transit papers to travel domestically, to board trains and airplanes, to go to college, even to perform routine chores of daily life. "It becomes a reward-punishment-type system, and you make your own calculation," explained Democrat operative Rahm Emanuel,[68] who attained notoriety for advising fellow Democrats to "never let a serious crisis go to waste."[69]

Indeed, Communist governments discovered long ago that the best way to control a population was through "a reward-punishment-type system"—benefits earned if people did what they were told, benefits denied if they did not. In totalitarian states such as the German Democratic Republic or Communist Czechoslovakia, people who failed to comply with government orders were often not overtly punished. Instead, disobedient or dissenting citizens simply saw their promotions denied, their children's applications for university rejected, their efforts to acquire a car stymied, long-planned vacation trips canceled.[70]

Historically, Americans reject this vision of total government control over their lives as the opposite of the freedoms they have fought and died to protect. But now the nation is divided and the Democrat Party and its followers have embraced a totalitarian vision and mentality. This has produced a resistance by patriotic Americans. By August 2021, nine states had enacted laws limiting or explicitly prohibiting vaccine mandates targeting employees of public schools or government agencies,[71] while six states passed laws banning vaccine mandates for schools,[72] and twenty-one passed laws banning vaccine passports like those in New York.[73]

Biden's response to these challenges was to portray himself as the nation's savior and his opponents as misinformed and misguided enemies of essential remedies for the nation's plight. On August 3, 2021, after Florida Governor Ron DeSantis rejected government-required vaccine passports, lockdowns, and mask mandates for his state, Biden made this plea: "We need leadership from everyone. And if some governors aren't willing to do the right thing to beat this pandemic, then they should allow businesses and universities who want to do the right thing to be able to do it. I say to these governors, 'Please help. But if you aren't going to help, at least get out of the way of people who are trying to do the right thing. Use your power to save lives.'"[74]

It was a claim that the federal government had a monopoly on the truth, despite the sea of contradictory statements and policies that had characterized from the beginning both the governments' approach and that of its critics to the pandemic. It was also a demonization of anyone dissenting from government orthodoxy as an enemy of the truth, as un-American a view as one could imagine.

To his credit, DeSantis did not back down but held his ground: "Joe Biden suggests that if you don't do lockdown policies, then you should 'get out of the way.' But let me tell you this: If you're coming after the rights of parents in Florida, I'm standing in your way. I'm not going to let you get away with it. If you're trying to deny kids a proper in-person education, I'm going to stand in your way and I'm going to stand up for the kids in Florida. If you're trying to restrict people, impose mandates, if you're trying to ruin their jobs and their livelihoods and their small business, if you are trying to lock people down, I am standing in your way and I'm standing for the people of Florida."[75]

During a television interview with Fox's Laura Ingraham, DeSantis spoke to the hypocrisy of Biden's claim to represent the truth about the crisis and to possess a monopoly on the virtuous way to deal with it. "This is a guy that ran for president saying he would shut down the virus. He was not going to shut down America or the economy. He would shut down the virus. Yet what is he doing? He is bringing in people from over 100 different countries across the southern border. Every variant on this planet—some we don't even know about—are absolutely coming into our country that way. . . . He is lecturing people about imposing Covid restrictions and lockdowns and not only doing nothing to stop the border surge but actually facilitating it."[76] And then, addressing the president directly, DeSantis said: "Why don't you do your job? Why don't you get this border secure? Until you do that, I don't want to hear a blip about Covid from you."[77]

It was a classic standoff—one that spoke to the heart of the political debate over whether the country would stand by its constitutional principles and traditions or, under the cover of a malleable crisis, transition to a one-party state that sought total control over the population.

7

Reimagining the World

WHILE AMERICANS CHAFED under the restrictions imposed during the pandemic, while they watched as their freedoms were eroded and their livelihoods destroyed, one powerful segment of society did not mourn. It celebrated. It welcomed the lockdowns, shortages, and restricted freedoms and viewed the entire crisis with something akin to elation and awe. They did so because all the deprivations of the fight against Covid were benefits to the environment and also test runs for the social controls essential to their socialist plans. The editors of the left-wing *Guardian* summed up the view of progressives everywhere: "The brakes placed on economic activities of many kinds, worldwide, have led to carbon emission cuts that would previously have been unthinkable. . . . What was once impossible—socialist, reckless—now turns out not to be, at all."[1] All true, unless one valued one's individual freedom and material well-being.

In February 2020, Democratic presidential primary candidate and mega–climate funder Tom Steyer welcomed the usurpation of individual freedom by an all-wise and omnipotent government as the key to saving the planet. Rather than hiding his authoritarian plans, as many progressive politicians do, Steyer boldly proclaimed them: "I will declare a state of emergency on climate on the first day of my presidency," he promised. "I will use the Executive emergency powers of the presidency to tell companies how they can generate electricity, what kind of cars they can build—on what schedule, what kind of buildings we're gonna have, how we are going to use our public lands. We need to rebuild this country in a climate-smart way . . . we don't have a choice on this."[2] This was the voice of a would-be dictator, not a candidate for the presidency of a 245-year-old republic.

Summing up the views of the pandemic enthusiasts, *Newsweek* magazine reported, "Scientists, activists and religious leaders ranging from Pope Francis to filmmaker Spike Lee are highlighting lockdown reductions in air pollution, and nature 'coming alive' as part of a larger call to permanently change industrial and economic behavior after Covid-19."[3] Or as one climate-activist professor put it: "Economic growth needs to be exchanged" for "planned austerity" and "whole system change."[4] In other words, a system that produces prosperity, brings greater choice, opportunity, and material well-being to Americans more than any other people in history needs to be sacrificed to a regime of "planned austerity" that suits the ideological agendas of the radical left. A more succinct definition of the "whole system change" radical Democrats are planning for America would be hard to come by.

Ambitions of the Green New Deal

The ambitions of what the Democrats have billed as a Green New Deal were even larger and more intrusive than Tom Steyer's plans. The spokesperson the Democrats chose for this plan was the strikingly shallow Alexandria Ocasio-Cortez, an admirer of Fidel Castro, the man who took one of the richest countries in Latin America and turned it into one of the poorest in less than a generation. To accomplish this feat, Castro turned Cuba into an island prison.

When Ocasio-Cortez announced the Green New Deal, it already had the support of 600 left-wing organizations and more than 40 Democrat senators and legislators, including veteran Democrat leader Edwin Markey of Massachusetts and radical financier George Soros.[5]

The goals of the Green New Deal included eliminating the oil and gas industry with no provision for replacing the 5.2 million lost jobs, or the billions in revenues, or the dominant global positions in energy this would deliver to America's mortal adversaries, Russia, Venezuela, China, and Iran. Other goals were even more bizarre, like the elimination of air travel, and cattle flatulence, which sent methane gas into the atmosphere.[6]

On the other hand, many of the green proposals had nothing to do with saving the environment and everything to do with imposing communist master plans on a passive populace. One item called for a single-payer health care system that would put the federal government in charge of the entire health care industry and eliminate individual freedom in choosing a doctor or an insurance plan.[7] Another called for guaranteeing jobs at a "living wage" to everyone in the United States.[8] That the intention was to make every citizen a ward of the state was made clear in the guarantee of "economic security for all who are unable or *unwilling* to work (emphasis added)."[9] This latter goal of creating a totally dependent non-working class was also encapsulated in proposals for a universal basic income, or UBI—money from the government for nothing.[10]

Only an ideological wish list can explain why Green New Dealers are opposed to nuclear power, which is a clean energy. They call for the decommissioning of all existing nuclear power plants, even though these plants account for 60 percent of carbon-free energy production and eliminating them would have a negative impact on the environment.[11] They have also proposed cutting the defense budget by half, a traditional priority of the anti-American left, and one that raises the question: Who is the enemy—fossil fuels or the United States?

Biden's cancellation of the Keystone Pipeline as one of his first acts in office provides another revealing anomaly.[12] The cancellation inflicted massive hardship on American workers and consumers. Overnight more than

11,000 workers and their families lost their income.[13] Democrats justified their sacrifice by the "urgent" threat fossil fuels pose to the climate. But at almost the same time, Biden gave a green light to Russia's Nord Stream gas pipeline, which Trump had stopped. This sealed not only German but European dependence on Russian oil and put money into the pocket of a hostile dictatorship. An *actively hostile* dictatorship: At the very moment Biden made this environmentally incomprehensible decision, the Kremlin was conducting massive cyberattacks against American businesses, disrupting the American economy and costing millions in ransom to repair. Biden's decision cannot be squared with a concern for American security or for climate change.

The same is true of manifold priorities and decisions that characterized the contested lockdowns and mandates during the Covid pandemic. Political agendas justified by alleged crisis emergencies ruled the day. The more permanent the crisis was projected to be, the better. Radical transformations can be justified by fear and implemented by the absolute power that fear confers on authority. Changing the world—or reimagining it—to solve crises real and fictional has therefore been the common theme of every ideological tyranny—Fascist, Nazi, and Communist—that has ravaged humanity in modern times.

"Whole system change"—this is the real agenda of all the climate-crisis schemes about which Americans allegedly "don't have a choice." But, of course, Americans do have a choice. The main polluters of the world, composing roughly a third of its population, are China and India. Both have refused to observe the restraints proposed in the Paris Climate Accord. Therefore, nothing America can do by itself will achieve the goals sought by the climate alarmists. On the other hand, instead of pursuing their system of "planned austerity," America could choose to further increase gross national product with its free-market economy and use its leverage to persuade India, China, and other resistant nations to change their destructive policies.

Posing an apocalyptic alternative—like planetary death—to rejecting the totalitarian restrictions of the Green New Deal has no practical rationale in terms of the environment. But it provides a necessary means to force an unacceptable "whole system change" on those who value their freedom and prosperity and who would challenge it if extinction were not the alternative. The apocalyptic climate crisis is the justifying rationale; the infrastructure of a totalitarian state is the result.

The Biggest, Most Destructive Spending Spree Ever

Democrats won a one vote majority in the Senate after the 2020 election. Within the parameters of the American political tradition, sweeping, society-changing legislation—Social Security and Medicare, for example—was always passed by large bipartisan majorities. This was true until the Affordable Care Act (aka Obamacare), legislation affecting one-sixth of the American economy that the radical Democrats deliberately passed without a single Republican vote, even though a dozen Republicans wanted to support it.

The legislative agenda with which the Biden radicals launched their administration was the largest, most expensive in American history. The grand radical plan to change the world included a $6 trillion one-year budget;[14] a $1.9 trillion "American Rescue Plan,"[15] a $2 trillion[16] and also a $3.5 trillion infrastructure proposal;[17] and a $1.8 trillion "American Families Plan,"[18] or $15.2 trillion and still counting.

How big is a trillion dollars? A stack of one billion one-dollar bills would be 67.9 miles high. A trillion one-dollar bills would reach 67,866 miles into space. A trillion one-dollar bills, *laid end to end*, would stretch 96,906,656 miles—further than the distance from the earth to the sun.[19]

One of the overseers of this unprecedented spending spree is Bernie Sanders, the most popular figure in the Democrat Party. The chair of the Senate Budget Committee is also a lifelong admirer of bankrupt communist economies and of the Cuban dictator whose crackpot Marxist planning decisions brought his country to its knees in less than a generation. It is a commentary all in itself on the Democrat approach to sound economic policy, which has dire implications for the country's financial future.

The actual tax revenues for FY 2020 were $3.86 trillion, which would mean that in order to pay for Biden's massive increase in government spending, massive economy-killing tax hikes would be required, along with the printing of hundreds of billions, if not trillions of un-backed, inflationary paper dollars.

The immediately manifest inflationary consequences of the Biden policies were in part the result of its deter-mination to put as many people as possible on the gov-ernment dole and pay them to not work. Under the $1.9 trillion American Rescue Plan, for example, unemployed persons were provided $300 a week in addition to other subsidies Congress had passed during the height of the pandemic. Businesses were forced to raise prices and wages to employ workers, though even these inflationary bribes didn't save them from closing when they failed. This created an odd situation in which businesses were going out of business during an economic recovery be-cause they couldn't find employees to keep them open. At the end of June 2021, there were a record 10.1 million job openings unfilled,[20] despite the fact that the unem-ployment rate was 5.9 percent[21] overall, 10.1 percent in the restaurant sector.[22]

Within Biden's first six months in office, inflation had already taken a heavy toll on working- and middle-class Americans. Gas prices had risen 33 percent; housing costs were up more than 23 percent; and meat prices were at record levels.[23] This erosion of the value of the dollar rep-resented a large tax on the middle-class, working-class, and poor Americans Biden had promised he would pro-tect, repeatedly saying that he would not raise taxes by one penny on individuals and families making less than $400,000 a year.[24] Like so many Biden promises, this one proved empty as well.

Stealth was the operative principle of the Biden radicals—as it is of radicals generally. Lying is a political necessity for radicals because by their very nature radical proposals are too extreme for the general population to accept. Democracies depend on transparency in government. But a common political strategy is to conceal the true nature of the legislation being proposed in order to limit public scrutiny of its contents. A prime example was provided by the Democrats multi-trillion-dollar infrastructure bills.

The dictionary defines *infrastructure* as "the basic physical and organizational structures and facilities (e.g. buildings, roads, power supplies) needed for the operation of a society or enterprise."[25] And so it was until the Biden radicals unveiled their bills. As described by CNN, the Biden infrastructure bill "would provide $400 billion to bolster caregiving for aging and disabled Americans. His plan would expand access to long-term care services under Medicaid, eliminating the wait list for hundreds of thousands of people. It would provide more opportunity for people to receive care at home through community-based services or from family members."[26] The infrastructure bill—a 2,700-page document that no one who voted on it had read—also included $3.5 billion for Indian health, $2 billion for the Environmental Protection Agency, $455 million for Fish & Wildlife, and $50 million to study ways to tax per-mile road usage. In the end, scarcely 10 percent of the infrastructure bill was actually devoted to infrastructure.[27]

The programs it funded may or may not be worthy of support. Putting tax meters on automobiles, for example—one of the items in the bill—strikes at one of the most basic American freedoms and would hurt the poorest Americans most. But sold as investments in infrastructure, these proposed uses of taxpayer monies never get exposed to the kind of debate that makes democracies preferable to societies ruled from the center and operating from the top down.

Under a barrage of criticisms from Republicans who derided the bill as a "socialist wish-list," the Democrats split their proposals into two bills, the second of which had a price tag of $3.5 trillion and was generally referred to as the "human infrastructure bill." This bill was described by the *NY Post* editorial board as "a horror aiming to turn America into the welfare state of Bernie Sanders' dreams. It would hike taxes on business and the wealthy to create multiple new entitlements: universal preschool, free community college, paid family and medical leave. It would expand Medicare benefits while reducing the program's eligibility age, dump more cash on 'green energy' subsidies—and even offer [illegal] immigrants green cards and permanent status."[28] It was described as "the largest expansion of federal welfare programs in 60 years" although no one could tell for sure because the bill was unavailable before the vote. On August 10 in the middle of the night, House Democrats passed the bill without a single Republican vote.

Perhaps the most far-reaching and revealing aspect of the deceptive Democrat bills was the Child Tax Credit

reform, which provides $300 for each child in a house-
hold. Billed by the Biden administration as "tax cuts for
America's workers and families," it is no such thing. As
the Heritage Foundation's Robert Rector explains:

"In reality, the plan would offer zero long-term tax relief to working families with children. Even in the short
term, some 74 percent of aid would go for cash grants to
families who owe no income tax; only 26 percent would
go for tax relief. But even this limited tax relief would be
temporary, ending in 2025. Rather than providing tax relief, most of the short-term and permanent provisions of
the plan would give cash grants to families who do not
work or work comparatively little. The plan would also
disproportionately assist nonmarried, rather than married, families."[29]

This latter priority reflects the radical left's war against
the family and highlights the chief problem with utopian
schemes: the detachment from reality that comes from
replacing the lessons of experience with ideological dog-
mas. Paying people for doing nothing is demoralizing and
dependency-creating, and it is the reason that trillions of
dollars in welfare payments over a quarter of a century
had no impact on the poverty level. This prompted the
1996 Clinton welfare reform, whose central feature was
imposing work requirements on recipients of government aid.

As Rector summarizes the impact of the reform: "The
results of this change were dramatic. Welfare dependence plummeted; employment surged. The child poverty rate, which had been frozen for nearly a quarter

century, dropped dramatically. Today, poverty among single-parent families is roughly 60 percent lower than it was before reform."[30]

In other words, contrary to the Biden administration's rhetoric, "the primary focus and sole permanent feature of [its] child allowance policy would be not tax relief but the elimination of all work requirements and work incentives from the current child credit program. In pursuing this change, the administration explicitly seeks to overturn the foundations of welfare reform established during the Clinton presidency"—in short, to set back the clock on welfare twenty-five years.[31]

Progressives and Reactionaries

This regressive plan exposes the central deception of the Biden regime, which is the claim that it is the most progressive administration ever. In reality, it is the most reactionary. The only sense in which the Biden policies and the Green New Deal can be said to be progressive is that they advance the agendas of a discredited radical ideology. Their real-world effects are to set back American progress—in race relations, in creating a productive economy, and in fostering an educated, fair-minded, law-abiding populace—fifty to a hundred years.

Progressive ideology is familiar as the communist vision of a future equality based on government coercion. People often forget that the "equity" that Democrats speak about so often is actually the proclaimed goal of Marxist totalitarians everywhere: They seek to use government power to force everyone to be "equal"—except, of course, for party leaders who are, as George Orwell explained in *Animal Farm*, more equal than others. The difference is one of words, not of ends.

Thus, one of the provisions of the Democrats' Infrastructure bill is to virtually double the capital gains tax rate from 20 percent to 39.6 percent in order to pay for handouts to the non-working population.[32] This would perhaps marginally increase income equality, but it would certainly damage the investment incentives that produce general prosperity. Raising corporate taxes as the Biden administration intends to do diminishes corporate competitiveness and shrinks the benefits their success brings to ordinary Americans. Behind every proposal to support debtors by cancelling debts, or punish landlords when tenants cannot afford their rent, is Marx's class war against society's achievers and benefactors.

This war is driven by feelings of envy and resentment, rather than a passion for justice. Socialism is theft. What is just about theft? The progressive goal, phrased as an ideal, is captured in Marx's famous standard for societies where this kind of social justice allegedly prevails: "From each according to his ability, to each according to his need."[33] But how much—and what?—does an individual actually *need*?

Democrat cities and states are paying from $40,000 to $100,000 to satisfy homeless individuals' supposed needs, with the result that homelessness is rapidly increasing and the homeless who refuse to or cannot work are becoming more aggressive and destructive. What homeless people may actually need are a reinstitution of vagrancy laws and relocation to institutions where their mental problems and substance addictions can be addressed in a safe environment and possibly resolved. Taking them off the streets and protecting them (and others) would seem the most humane way to deal with the problem— not renting them expensive hotel rooms, which is the policy of the left.

By the same token, what can "from each according to his ability" mean in practice? What incentive is required to motivate an individual to build a Microsoft or a Tesla? Socialists have no answer, because they are unconcerned with human motivations and incentives, as they are with human character generally. Otherwise, they would not be relentlessly providing incentives to the shiftless and failed segments of society to stop working, continue their destructive habits, and make no effort to improve their skills or expand their capabilities. Nor would Democrats be so thoughtlessly intent on punishing the movers and shakers of a new world of increased prosperity and conveniences. Truly progressive solutions would be rewards for achievement and effort. Tolerance and encouragement for spongers, leeches, and self-destructive individuals would not.

Marxism—now camouflaged and rebranded as progressivism—is a reactionary creed that has been discredited over and over again, and without exception, over the century in which it has been put into practice. These failed experiments in equality, implemented from Russia to Cambodia, have resulted in the deaths of more than

100 million people at the hands of their own governments. Their crimes were always the same: resisting the life-crippling schemes that were put forth in the name of progressive social justice. As a nation founded by conservative realists, America has provided a counter-example: how a nation based on sound observations of human character can thrive and be a magnet for would-be immigrants from all over the world. America's founders, like its constitutional architect James Madison, understood from the beginning what fostering a socially creative and productive citizenry requires, which is the exact opposite of what Marxists and Democrats propose.

For example, in proposing measures to thwart the schemes of radical factions, Madison was describing the precise themes of the progressive agenda: "A rage for paper money, for an abolition of debts, for an equal division of property, or for any other improper or wicked project," as he put it. These destructive causes, Madison wrote, would "be less apt to pervade the whole body of the Union" if America had a system of checks and balances to protect minorities and prevent the establishment of a tyranny of the majority.[34]

8

Orwellian Acts

PROGRESSIVES SEEK A fundamental transformation of society that, they claim, would establish peace, justice, and equity as the orders of the day. Why, then, have they killed so many people in peacetime, and taken away the freedom of so many others in gulags and concentration camps? This is a question that is better examined before American radicals achieve a one-party state than after.

The answer to the question should be obvious. When a righteous elite becomes a party powered by hatred and marches in lockstep toward its ideological goal, and when this same party sets out to transform society into a politically correct realm, there is no limit to the control they will require to achieve the perfection for which they strive. There will always be another politically incorrect deviant who needs to be cancelled, another microaggression that needs to be punished, another dissent that needs to be suppressed.

Already, radicals in America and the West have sought to criminalize certain uses of ordinary pronouns to satisfy the woke sensibilities of the LGBTQI left. Already, the Biden Democrats have asserted their right to strip property-owning landlords of what may have taken them a lifetime to earn and to transfer their wealth to those who haven't worked as hard or achieved as much. All in the name of justice. Already, if you are white but fail to concede to a workplace diversity trainer that your skin color makes you a white supremacist, you are facing the loss of a job and possibly a career. Already, the party of righteous Democrats is planning to impose internal passports on the entire population, putting its freedom of movement and access to services under the government's thumb. Moreover, all these tyrannical ambitions are within reach for a party with a mere one-vote majority in a Congress composed of 535 members and in a country deeply divided on the issues of life, liberty, and the pursuit of happiness. Such is the awesome and terrifying power of an ideological zeal justified by planetary crises and mostly imagined social inequities.

The Equality Act

Even before Biden's election, House Speaker Pelosi had set the agenda of the 117th Congress with two major pieces of legislation designed to advance the cause of a totalitarian state. One of these laws she deceptively named The Equality Act, presenting it in these pious terms:

"Our nation was founded on the promise that all are created equal and are worthy of dignity and respect, regardless of who they are or whom they love. With the reintroduction of The Equality Act, Congressional Democrats are making a resounding commitment to this truth: that all Americans must be treated equally under the law, not just in the workplace, but in every place. The Democratic House will now swiftly pass this landmark legislation and will keep working until it is finally enacted into law—so that we can combat anti-LGBTQ discrimination that undermines our democracy and advance justice in America."[1]

Listening to these words, one would never know that The Equality Act is in fact legislation that would destroy the most basic American right, and the foundation of all other rights guaranteed by the Constitution: the freedom of thought. *War is peace! Freedom is slavery!* Orwell himself could not have improved on Pelosi's doublespeak.

The Equality Act is ostensibly a measure to extend the antidiscrimination provisions of the civil rights acts to include sexual orientation and gender identity. But it is, in fact, a law aimed at resolving some of the most contentious issues in American life—abortion and transgenderism—by government decree; it is a proposal to resolve these contentious issues by giving the extremist views of Pelosi and her zealots the force of law. In effect, The Equality Act arrogates to government the power to redefine what it is to be a man or a woman for all Americans and to do so behind a one-vote majority in the Senate.

The justification for the law is that it is based on science and truth. In fact, the transgender theories behind The Equality Act fly in the face of established medical theory and practice. As the Heritage Foundation's Emilie Kao explains:

"Because gender theory asserts that the body can be amended to match self-perception, doctors treat gender dysphoria unlike other disorders related to body image. . . . With other mental disorders, doctors seek to address the underlying problems that have led to an inaccurate or harmful self-image. Normally, doctors and counselors don't affirm the distorted self-images of their patients. Rather than telling girls who like sports and the outdoors to undergo permanent disfiguration, counselors and doctors could expand the parameters of girlhood beyond dresses and baking. And boys who like the arts and fashion could be accepted as they are, not told that they are girls trapped in the wrong body."[2]

As in other areas of radical transformation, there is a lot of complexity to the transgender issue that its proponents want to suppress. Most fundamentally, there is no scientific basis for transgenderism.[3] The concept that women are trapped in men's bodies and vice versa is based on speculation, not on identifiable biological processes. In fact, for large numbers of those who come to identify as transgender and undergo the transition, the procedures do not resolve the psychological issues that led them to transition in the first place. Large numbers of those who do undergo the transition express regret afterward. Equally disturbing numbers commit suicide.[4]

The problem with the Democrats' ram-it-through approach as applied to government authority is that an overwhelming majority of Americans don't think gender is a choice and don't think underage children should be subjected to medical puberty blockers as part of a gender transition that would alter their lives forever.

Nor do they feel comfortable with legislation that would prevent religious Americans from practicing their faith. Under The Equality Act, religious hospitals, and doctors generally, would be required against their better judgment and religious beliefs to perform mastectomies on teenage girls suffering from "gender dysphoria." The ideological left is already extremely intolerant of those who disagree with them, as demonstrated by the nine-year persecution of a Colorado baker for refusing to decorate a cake celebrating "gay marriage and gender transition." Under The Equality Act, Catholic hospitals and caregivers who refuse to perform abortions because of the tenets of their faith would be violating the law.

Outlawing the free expression of religious conscience is a direct violation of the First Amendment, the cornerstone of American democracy. Yet Democrats, backed by the Obama and Biden White Houses, have been pursuing, persecuting, and punishing Catholic institutions like the Little Sisters of the Poor for decades. The Equality Act would complete the job of destroying them altogether.

The Orwellian overtones of this legislation are deafening. The Democrats have presented their bill as a key legislation designed to provide a basic American right—equality—to all Americans. But in fact, The Equality Act denies the most basic American right to all Americans who disagree with it.

The problem with the Democrats' claim that they are merely extending the civil rights legislation that ended segregation in the South and racial discrimination throughout the United States is this: By the time that legislation was passed, it was supported by the overwhelming majority of the American people. In Congress, the Civil Rights Act of 1964 passed by an overwhelming majority of 363 to 157. Seventy-eight percent of the "no" vote in the Senate was cast by Democrats who attempted to block the Act by filibuster and whose ranks included the southern segregationists.[5] Seventy-four percent of the "no" vote in the House was cast by Democrats.[6]

Inspired by America's WWII victory against a "master race" and by a nonviolent Civil Rights movement organized to create a "color-blind" society, Americans as a people had come to the conclusion that racial discrimination had no place in American life. No such vision or consensus exists where transgenderism or abortion are concerned. Instead, divisive passions, partisan legislation, and government coercion are the orders of the day—a prescription for tearing the country apart.

The Democrats' One Vote Majority

In a democracy, electoral majorities are the ruling authorities. Consequently, Democrats have for decades focused their energies on reshaping the electoral map. Opening the southern border in the midst of a global pandemic was one catastrophic strategy for achieving this. With equal recklessness, Democrats have focused on rigging the voting process itself. They did this most blatantly through campaigns involving thousands of operatives to reverse the recommendations of the 2005 bipartisan Carter-Baker Commission on Federal Electoral Reform.[7] In other words, by systematically changing the election laws to make it easier to cheat.

On the final day of the 2020 election, Republicans held a two-person majority in the Senate. This would have allowed them to block the entire legislative Democrat agenda and stop its transformation of the American economy and social order into a massive welfare state with the government intruding into every aspect of its citizens' lives. They could have prevented the invasion of the country by millions of illegal migrants from over 100 countries under the auspices of billion-dollar drug cartels smuggling in record levels of fentanyl and other deadly drugs supplied by the Chinese. They could have stopped hundreds of thousands of Covid carriers, and tens of thousands of convicted felons, all invisible to government authorities and their future victims, from making America their home.

This Republican firewall depended on the reelection of two Georgia Republican senators—David Perdue and Kelly Loeffler—who had failed to achieve more than 50 percent of the vote and were facing a run-off challenge from two Democrat radicals—Raphael Warnock and Jon Ossoff. Both won their run-offs, allowing the most radical transformation of the American economy and social order to go ahead by a margin of 1 percent.[8]

Biden had won the general election in the red state of Georgia by a final tally of 11,779 votes out of approximately 5 million ballots cast—0.25 percent of the vote.[9] Republicans had strenuously protested the result. The 2005 Carter-Baker Commission had advised all U.S. states that to guarantee free and fair elections, they should increase their voter ID requirements and minimize the use of mail-in ballots, which "remain the largest source of potential voter fraud."[10] But in both the November 2020 elections and the January 2021 Senate runoff elections, Georgia greatly relaxed ID requirements for the massive number of people who were voting by mail. This was enormously significant, in light of the fact that Georgians cast more than 1 million mail-in ballots in the November 2020 elections and in each of the January 2021 Senate runoff elections, where the final margins were also razor-thin.[11]

How did Georgia come to alter its election rules in the year of a crucial presidential election? On March 6, 2020, its Republican Secretary of State—an anti-Trump Republican named Brad Raffensperger—signed a consent decree with officials from the Democrat Party of Georgia, the Democrat Senatorial Campaign Committee, and the Democrat Congressional Campaign Committee. Through this decree he entered "a Compromise Settlement Agreement and Release." That agreement changed the statutory requirements—as they had been set forth in Georgia CODE § 21-2-386(a)(1)(B).71—for verifying signatures on absentee ballot envelopes in order to confirm the voter's identity.[12]

The key Democrat player in this crucial arrangement was Marc Elias of the Perkins Coie law firm in Washington, D.C. Elias had previously served as chief counsel to both the Hillary Clinton 2016 presidential campaign and the Democratic National Committee and had been a key player in the Russiagate hoax that fueled two failed attempts to remove President Trump from office with the help of the KGB.[13]

Republicans protested that the Georgia arrangement was clearly unconstitutional. The U.S. Constitution specifies that election rules are set by the legislatures of the states, not by officials like Georgia Secretary of State Raffesnsperger.[14] But their protests were to no avail. The same unconstitutional rules were in place for the January 5 run-off.

The apparent corruption that had taken place in the 2020 elections had the obvious effect of demoralizing Republican voters when the runoffs were held in January 2021. Republicans' frustration over what they viewed as a rigged election led to a massive dropout among Republican voters, who refused to participate in the January 5 election. An analysis by *The Atlanta Journal-Constitution* found that after Warnock and Ossoff qualified for the January run-offs, (a) more than 752,000 Georgia voters who had cast ballots in the November 2020 elections did not vote again, and (b) more than half of the January no-shows were white, and many of them lived in rural areas, constituencies that typically tended to vote Republican. As one dispirited Georgia Republican said after deciding not to vote in the runoffs: "What good would it have done to vote? They have votes that got changed. I don't know if I'll ever vote again."[15]

In Georgia, where Biden's final margin of victory was a mere 11,779 votes, Trump and his legal team claimed that illegal ballots had been cast by or in the name of (a) more than 2,500 felons, (b) 66,247 underage voters, (c) 2,423 unregistered voters, (d) 4,926 individuals who had failed to register prior to the state's voter-registration deadline, (e) 395 individuals who voted in Georgia and one additional state, (f) 40,279 people who had moved across county lines in Georgia without re-registering in their new county of residence, (g) 30,000 to 40,000 people whose absentee ballots lacked a valid, verifiable signature, (h) 20,311 voters who had moved out of state and thus were no longer eligible to vote in Georgia, and (i) 10,315 people who were dead.[16]

Attempting to Remedy the Problem

Having given up the field to the Democrat election fixers and lost the national election, Republicans could no longer deny the gravity of what had taken place. All over the country, Republicans who had let Trump wage the battle for election integrity virtually alone now engaged in efforts to prevent the 2020 loss from becoming the permanent fixture of a one-party state. Georgia Republicans in the eye of the storm took the lead. They formed a Georgia Special Committee on Election Integrity and created the Election Integrity Act of 2021.[17] It was passed on party-line votes by both chambers of the Georgia legislature on March 25 and signed into law by Republican Governor Brian Kemp later that same day.

Democrats immediately denounced the new law as an expression of Republican white supremacy and an attempt to suppress the black vote. President Biden summed up the party line in particularly inept fashion: "This makes Jim Crow look like Jim Eagle."[18] And then as a clarification: "Jim Crow on steroids."[19] Democrat activist and failed Georgia gubernatorial candidate Stacey Abrams led the Democrats' charge that Republicans were white supremacists determined "to thwart an increase in voting by people of color by constricting, removing, or otherwise harming their ability" to cast their ballots.[20] Massachusetts Senator Elizabeth Warren concurred: "The Republican who is sitting in Stacey Abrams' chair just signed a despicable voter suppression bill into law to take Georgia back to Jim Crow."[21]

A key provision of the reform bill was a new voter ID requirement for absentee/mail-in ballots. This measure plugged a hole in existing Georgia ID laws, dating back to 2008. Georgia election law had already established clearly defined voter ID standards for all in-person voting. But this left a loophole for fraud when Democrats were able to institute massive mail-in ballots using the Covid crisis as a pretext.[22]

Georgia's election laws provided voter ID documents free of charge to any Georgia resident who might desire one.[23] In the other words, there was no racial element to voter ID requirements in Georgia, whether for in-person or mail-in balloting. Democrat claims that the new law was a return to the Jim Crow South, when blacks were denied the right to vote, was just another Democrat fraud. Before the new law, absentee mail-in ballots had been sent to anyone who requested them, with no measures taken to verify the voter's identity. Obviously, the potential for fraud in such circumstances was great.[24]

Since ID credentials were provided free to every Georgia citizen through the new reform, the argument that voter suppression was being performed through lack of funds was baseless. Under the new reform law, Georgia allows its citizens to use their social security number, their driver's license number, their state ID number, a copy of a current utility bill, a bank statement, a paycheck or government check made out in their name, or any other government document showing their name and address for voting purposes.[25] In pretending that the new Georgia law was an attempt to suppress the black vote, the Democrats reached a new level of brazenness.

The Democrats' opposition to what was a mild, non-discriminatory reform quickly escalated until it became a spectacle in itself. Like officials in other states, the Georgia legislators sought to prevent political solicitation within 150 feet of a polling place, or 25 feet of any voters waiting in line to cast their ballots. These were the distances required for anyone seeking to provide a glass of water for voters waiting in line.[26]

This innocuous provision was immediately misrepresented by the Democrat critics as a malicious plot to deny humane relief from the heat to voters they regarded as racial inferiors. "It's an atrocity," railed President Biden, who continued to refer to the Georgia reform as Jim Crow 2. "You don't need anything else to know that this is nothing but a punitive design to keep people from voting. You can't provide water for people about to vote? Give me a break."[27] Actually, the law did allow the voters themselves to get water if they needed it, and also to receive drinks from nonpartisan election officials.

Major corporations supported the Democrats' attacks on the Georgia voting reform as a bid to turn the racial clock back sixty years. The Major League Baseball Association announced it was moving the previously scheduled All-Star Game from Atlanta to Denver, and the Biden Department of Justice filed a Civil Rights suit against the state of Georgia. The move of the All-Star game was a particularly hypocritical travesty, depriving an African American–run city, with a majority African American population, of an estimated $100 million in revenues. And to do so because of an election law that was less restrictive than the law in Joe Biden's home state.[28]

The *For the People Act*

Increasingly desperate Democrats knew that their attempts to discredit and bury the opposition to their "transformative" schemes could not be accomplished by a one-vote majority, which might be reversed in the next turn of the election cycle. Their plans to prevent this by securing a permanent majority were the focus of Pelosi's other major piece of legislation—the For the People Act.

The American founders had attempted to block sinister ambitions like seeking a permanent majority by placing control of elections in the hands of state legislatures. Decentralized power, they reasoned, would be more difficult to manipulate and control. By the year 2021 this meant the elected legislators in all fifty states.

The For the People Act was designed to undo this constitutional arrangement by federalizing election rules and requiring candidates to depend on federal funding. It would put the levers of electoral control as far as possible from the people. And as close to the levers of power in an overwhelming Democrat city and bureaucracy.

The For the People Act would also reverse the major recommendations of the bipartisan Carter-Baker Commission to prevent voter theft. Specifically, it would outlaw voter ID requirements and allow all voting to be by mail-in ballots.[29]

The Act was passed by the votes of 220 Democrats in the House of Representatives. Not a single Republican voted aye.[30]

The Revolution Must Go On!

At the same time the Department of Justice suit against Georgia's voter reform was pending, Democrat members of Congress were demonstrating at State Capitols across the country to protest inaction on the For the People Act, filibuster reform, and similar legislation—and getting arrested for doing so.[31] MSNBC host Rachel Maddow invited former President Barack Obama's attorney general, Eric Holder, to comment. "[Protesters] needed to be 'in the street,'" he said, "and 'getting arrested' in the political fight over voting laws."[32]

It was an odd comment for a former attorney general, someone presumably committed to upholding the rule of law. But it perfectly captured the problem the nation faced at the hands of radical lawmakers committed to overthrowing the law and to urging others to do so as well.

"What do you make of the direct-action strategy that is being brought by voting rights advocates?" Maddow asked Holder. "Obviously, Vice President Harris and President Biden are very much in support of the reforms like the For the People Act, and they've advocated for it. We know that. We've heard all the speeches. We know their position. Yet you're seeing increasingly relentless focus by moral leaders getting arrested at the Senate office building, at the Supreme Court, at the White House."

"Power concedes nothing without demand," Holder replied, employing a mischievous cliché of the radical left. "Raising the consciousness of people by demonstrating, by getting arrested, by doing the things that ended segregation. . . . Citizens need to be calling representatives to demand the kind of change that will make this country more representative, make our democracy more fair."[33]

It was a surreal comment perfectly reflective of the historical moment. The president and vice president of the United States were Democrats who supported the legislation the protesters were demanding. By vast margins, Americans supported the Voting Rights Act and equality for blacks before the law. How did this justify criminal acts—and criminal acts advocated by the former chief law enforcement officer of the nation? The criminal acts were designed to prevent the legal system from working its course. Patience was a necessity in a democracy—as was submitting to the rule of law. By breaking the law and demonizing one's opposition, radicals like Holder and the Obama-Biden Democrats were threatening the whole edifice of the democracy that put them in power.

9

The Fall of Afghanistan

"*Not even during the Civil War did insurrectionists breach the Capitol of the United States of America, the citadel of our democracy. Not even then. But on January the 6, 2021, they did.*"

These were the words Joe Biden used to address a special signing ceremony on August 5, 2021. The ceremony was for the Congressional Gold Medal awards to Capitol police officers who defended the Capitol on January 6.

But were his words commensurate with the facts? Did a battalion of insurrectionists attack the Capitol? Was it an invading army comparable to the Confederate forces? What we do know is this: On January 6, about 600 unarmed, middle-aged protesters mostly walked through the unguarded front door of the Capitol, broke a window or two, and scuffled with an under-manned Capitol Police force that had difficulty containing them. Some of the scuffles were violent. But video surveillance footage of the entry shows large numbers of middle-aged protesters walking politely between velvet ropes, guided by police, taking selfies as they went.

Six months earlier, General Mark Milley, chairman of the Joint Chiefs of Staff, had had a confrontation with Trump adviser Stephen Miller in the White House. The issue was the president's request to invoke the Insurrection Act to send troops to protect the White House, which was being threatened by a Black Lives Matter mob. The mob had already torched the Church of the Presidents in Lafayette Square and the gatehouse along the White House fence. Trump was requesting an invocation of the Insurrection Act and federal troops to restore order. His aide was arguing that this mob, accompanied by hundreds of lawless others, justified the request.

Sources present described the scene. Taking a dramatic pause, "Milley turned toward the president and pointed at the painting of Lincoln that hung on the wall to the right of the Resolute Desk. 'Mr. President,' he said, 'that guy had an insurrection. You don't have an insurrection. When guys show up in gray and start bombing Fort Sumter, you'll have an insurrection. I'll let you know about it. You don't have an insurrection right now.'" Milley was later revealed as an anti-Trump zealot, and didn't maintain this position when the shoe was on the other foot. When President Biden and Speaker Pelosi were waging their war on Trump in August 2021 over the alleged insurrection on January 6, he remained dutifully and irresponsibly silent[1] amid their overwrought claims.

Nor was the alleged insurrection of January 6 the worst breach of the Capitol in the history of the Republic, as Biden, Pelosi, and their media chorus maintained. Not by a long shot. On March 1, 1954, four Puerto Rican terrorists armed with automatic pistols shot thirty rounds at representatives from the gallery of the House. Five members of Congress were wounded, one seriously. The attackers were arrested and then convicted in federal court. They were found guilty and given sentences that amounted to life in prison. In 1978 and 1979, their sentences were commuted by President Jimmy Carter and all four returned to Puerto Rico.

Pelosi's Show Trial

The January 6 protesters carried no firearms and shot no one. Did anyone seriously think the most powerful government in the world was threatened by these protesters, many of them middle aged, some dressed up in face paint and wearing buffalo horns? Videos taken during the events show many of the protesters chatting amiably with police. Yet from the very beginning, Nancy Pelosi and the Democrats were determined to use this protest against their abuses of authority as an excuse to crack down on their political opponents and demonize them as "domestic terrorists." And this time General Milley was not only silent but enabled the crackdown when Pelosi ringed the Capitol with 25,000 troops to meet a nonexistent threat.

Sixth months after the January 6 protest, with demonstrators charged with trespassing still locked up in jail, Pelosi began her weekly news conference with these words: "This morning, with great solemnity and sadness, I'm announcing that the House will be establishing a select committee on the Jan. 6 insurrection. A temple of our democracy was attacked by insurrectionists. It is imperative that we seek the truth as to what happened."[2]

But, of course, like the dictator she had become, Pelosi had just told the media her distorted version of the truth. As was obvious from all her pronouncements, committees, and impeachments of late, Pelosi had no interest whatsoever in exploring two sides to even the most consequential matters of state. To Pelosi, democracy and the Constitution were just rhetorical sledgehammers with which to beat her opponents into submission. Her January 6 inquiry wasn't about an impartial search for the facts of what had taken place. It was about pursuing her scorched-earth strategy against the defeated president and his followers and convicting them of treason.

Pelosi's committee wasn't going to explore why the Capitol Police were insufficiently prepared for what they had been informed would happen. It wasn't going to ask about what the fifty FBI contacts and military personnel who got arrested inside the Capitol were up to that day. It wasn't going to look into the killing of an unarmed military veteran, Ashli Babbitt, or ask why Pelosi herself was protecting the identity of the officer who shot her and whom she had already decided behind closed doors wasn't guilty of a crime. Instead, it was going to convict

Donald Trump of inciting an insurrection, and was going to do so despite the findings of the FBI that only a handful of those present were part of a network coordinating the protest, and none were linked to the president.

Everyone knew the verdict of Pelosi's hand-picked "commission" in advance because Pelosi had already launched a failed and unconstitutional impeachment of Trump, charging him with inciting an insurrection on January 6. She was not about to permit a conclusion that exposed her abuse of power and her hate-fueled vendetta for what it was. Nancy Pelosi was the very embodiment of the ambition to establish a tyranny of the majority that the Founders feared.

Consequently, no one was surprised when she broke all precedent by rejecting the first two Republicans House Minority leader Kevin McCarthy proposed for what was supposed to be a bipartisan body. And no one was surprised when she selected for her committee nine members of Congress—including two Republicans—who, to a man and a woman, had voted to impeach Trump on the very charge they were going to investigate.

Trump the Target Forever!

For five years, Pelosi had led Democrats in their attempts to convict, remove, and erase Donald Trump for alleged crimes against the Constitution, against the country, and against common decency, and had failed. By now most people not affected by Trump hysteria had concluded that in all these efforts, the target was not really Trump himself but the party he led, the country he put first, and the record 74 million voters who still supported him despite all the attacks.

By ignoring these voters and dismissing them as racists, the Democrats had effectively told them their votes did not count—and would never count. This was made apparent by the reactions of the Democrats to Ron DeSantis, a rising Republican star. The Florida governor had implemented the border and Covid-19 policies embraced by Trump supporters and had shown himself to be a fighter in Trump's mold. The Democrats' reaction to his rising popularity was to characterize him as "more dangerous than Trump," which showed that as far as they were concerned, Trump would continue to function as a bar to judge, and a whipping boy to dismiss any Republican who reflected the views of the movement that Trump had called into being.[3]

Demonizing Trump was—and had been for more than five years—the Democrats' chief political weapon in their relentless drive to create a one-party state. Demonizing Trump and his followers laid the necessary groundwork for a political system in which dissenters were rendered powerless, and "bipartisanship" an empty promise.

If Democrats could still deploy Trump-hatred and serial slanders of Republicans as "white supremacists," "patriotic extremists," and "violent insurrectionists," and use them to win the 2022 midterms, they would be in a position to secure the provisions of the For the People Act—to federalize elections, to make mail-in balloting the law nationwide, to outlaw voter IDs, to enforce open borders, to change the electoral map, to abolish the Electoral College, to pack the Supreme Court, and to establish that tyranny of the majority they had spent so much political capital to achieve.

On the other hand, if Republicans supporting America-first policies, secure borders, free markets, law and order, and a color-blind society won the midterms, the Democrats' entire nation-transforming agenda would go down in defeat. And every indicator—past and present—was pointing toward a Republican landslide, which would accomplish just that.

A Politicized Defense Establishment

In these circumstances and given their encouragement of criminals, contempt for the law, and disregard for the Constitution, what were Democrats capable of and what might they do?

Unfortunately, the Democrats' behavior in the previous two elections and throughout the summer of violent insurrections provided ominous clues. Equally disturbing was the way the Obama-Biden administration had politicized the intelligence and military establishments to the point that neither could be trusted to defend the Constitution or the integrity of a presidential vote.

In 2015, abetted by the intelligence agencies, the FBI launched a plot to block a Trump election victory. When that failed, they launched a two-year attempt to overthrow the Trump presidency with fabricated charges that he had colluded with Russia to rig the vote.[4] This hoax—exposed by Congressman Devin Nunes and the $35 million Mueller investigation—has never been repudiated by the Democrat Party or by Democrats on the intelligence committee who spread the hoax. Nor has any Intelligence official paid a reasonable price for participating in these treasonous acts.

The military's attitude toward the 2020 election has received less attention but contains even more ominous indications. Biden's Secretary of Defense, Lloyd Austin, is the first African American to hold the position. He is also a Black Lives Matter Trump-hater who has required Critical Race Theory training for all military personnel. As one of his first acts in office, Austin ordered a two-month military stand-down so that his like-minded agents could conduct a witch hunt for "domestic terrorists"—namely Republicans, conservatives, and critics of Black Lives Matter in the military ranks. The training materials Austin has imposed on military recruits include videos lionizing Democrat presidents like Obama and Clinton as civil rights heroes but omitting the gains made by black, Asian, and Hispanic Americans under Trump. These inevitably sow seeds of division in the ranks. And when a maliciously false history of America as a nation born in slavery in 1619 is presented as truth, and the true American founding in 1776 as an avatar of equality and freedom is erased, the consequences for the morale of America's defenders are obviously destructive and dangerous.[5]

In his first days as Secretary of Defense, Austin ordered hundreds of former President Trump's appointees from at least thirty-one Pentagon advisory boards and pan-els to resign. On April 9, 2021, Secretary Austin issued a memorandum announcing the establishment of the Countering Extremism Working Group to spearhead the military's witch hunt designed to locate and stamp out wrongthink ("extremism") in its ranks.[6]

To lead the Group, Austin appointed as his senior ad-viser on Human Capital and Diversity, Equity, and Inclu-sion a black American named Bishop Garrison, who has made no secret of his profound contempt for Trump and the scores of millions of people who voted for him. In July 2019, for example, Garrison said in a tweet: "Support for him [Trump], a racist, is support for ALL his beliefs. He's dragging a lot of bad actors (misogynist, extremists, other racists) out into the light, normalizing their actions. If you support the President, you support that. There is no room for nuance with this." In other words, cancel the 74 million Americans who voted for Trump. This is the man Lloyd Austin put in charge of purifying the military.[7]

Austin and the Biden administration decided that in order to help them determine who is, or is not, a dan-gerous extremist, they would rely on the judgment of the Southern Poverty Law Center (SPLC)—a notorious fact-challenged smear operation that routinely conflates traditional, respectable conservative organizations like the Family Research Council and the American Enter-prise Institute with fascist, skinhead, and neo-Nazi fringe groups. Ben Carson, Ayaan Hirsi Ali, and other defenders of human rights and civility have been defamed by the SPLC as "hate-mongers."[8] In recent years, the SPLC has been revealed as a race-hustling shakedown racket when both its founder and president were forced to resign amid accusations by former staffers of overt sexual harassment and racism.

One of the first casualties of Austin's witch hunt was a Space Force commander named Matthew Lohmeier, a fifteen-year veteran whose unit was tasked with locating Ballistic Missile launches. Lohmeier's command was terminated because he self-published a book, *Irresistible Revolution*, documenting the military's backing for Cultural Marxist doctrines that divided the troops by race and denounced America as a white supremacist nation. Lohmeier gave evidence of the demoralizing effects of these pernicious doctrines on the young men and women who had volunteered to defend their country but were now having second thoughts.[9] The military's response to this reasonable critique was to terminate Lohmeier's military career and deny him his pension.

The problem with a politicized military command was evident when the White House tried to invoke the Insurrection Act back in June 2020. If the request had been accepted by the military, it would have ended a nationwide reign of terror by putting troops on the street. Instead, as a result of Milley's decision, the situation in Lafayette Square grew so bad that the Park Police decided to clear the protesters out.

After the protest was broken up and Milley was seen with Trump crossing Lafayette Square in the aftermath, Milley quickly withered under attacks by the anti-Trump press. "I should not have been there," Milley mumbled in an apology video. He then defended the thousands of acts of arson, mass pillaging, and even murder that occurred throughout 2020 by privileged young people as responses to "centuries of injustice toward African Americans."[10] He made clear that he was not going to be an unbiased enforcer of the law, and also that his allegiance was not to his commander-in-chief.[11]

A National Humiliation and Defeat

As chairman of the Joint Chiefs of Staff, General Mark Milley was at the center of the planning for America's withdrawal from Afghanistan, where American forces and their NATO allies had been battling the Taliban and associated terrorist groups for twenty years. During that time, in addition to controlling the major cities and thwarting Taliban attacks, the allies had been involved in "nation building," an attempt to create a modern society with modern attitudes toward women in a country ruled by bloodthirsty terrorists whose holy scripture instructed them to beat and kill women for expressing themselves, and behead religious infidels. The attitudes of the Taliban were generally rooted in barbaric seventh-century beliefs.

During those twenty years, hundreds of thousands of Afghans had been involved in activities that ranged from assisting the American military to encouraging women to engage in practices such as renouncing their burkas or going to college—under Taliban rule punishable by death. Consequently, any withdrawal of American forces confronted a daunting humanitarian challenge: to evacuate

American citizens, Afghans who had aided the American effort, and Afghan women who had participated in activities the Taliban had forbidden to them. Those women would find their freedoms sorely diminished or would be turned into sex slaves or murdered if they were left behind. As the Taliban was no respecter of women or children, their families would have to be evacuated too.

On April 14, 2021, Biden announced that he intended to adhere to Trump's withdrawal date of May 1 and complete the process by September 11, the twentieth anniversary of the 9/11 attacks.[12] The selection of that date, as though in celebration of America's twin defeats at the hands of the Taliban, produced enough of an uproar to cause Biden to change the withdrawal date to August 31.[13]

One wouldn't have to attend a military academy to know that a mission whose primary purpose was an evacuation of so many civilians would have to take place in two stages: first, the evacuation of the civilians in need of rescue, and second, the military who would have stayed to protect them. Biden, apparently with the support of his generals, reversed the order and began withdrawing troops and abandoning American airfields and bases before the rescue operation had even gotten under way.

This course of action was central to what happened next. Withdrawal of American air cover and intelligence deprived the Afghan military of the strategic advantages that had allowed it to fend off the Taliban terrorists thus far. The result was a rapid collapse of any military resistance to the Taliban forces. While Biden assured everyone the Taliban were at least six months to two years away from taking Kabul and the whole country, this nightmare was only weeks away.[14] As the military tide began turning, Biden continued to insist that the country would not fall, although he did so knowing that he was lying. In a private July 23 phone call whose contents came into Reuters' possession, he said to Afghanistan's president Ashraf Ghani: "I need not tell you the perception around the world and in parts of Afghanistan, I believe, is that things are not going well in terms of the fight against the Taliban," Biden said. "And there is a need, *whether it is true or not*, there is a need to project a different picture" (emphasis added).[15]

Previously, on July 8, with total defeat a month away, he declared that "the likelihood there's going to be the Taliban overrunning everything and owning the whole country is highly unlikely."[16] He could not have been more wrong. Without American air cover and intelligence support, the Afghan government forces collapsed in a matter of weeks. On August 15, the Afghan president fled the country, and hours later the Taliban took Kabul.[17]

From the outset, one of the main strategic questions facing the planners of the American withdrawal was the fate of the Bagram Air Base. It housed the largest airfield in the country—crucial for the evacuation. Moreover, it was defensible in a way the Kabul airport was not. The Bagram Air Base also housed the largest prison in Afghanistan, which was filled with 5,000 to 7,000 hardened terrorist fighters for the Taliban, ISIS, and al-Qaeda.[18]

For reasons that will forever remain inexplicable, the decision of Biden and his acquiescing generals was to abandon Bagram without even notifying the commander of the base until the abandonment was complete. In the overnight hours of July 2, the United States left Bagram and its weapon arsenal for the terrorists and did so by quietly shutting off the electricity. They didn't even notify the base's new Afghan commander, Gen. Mir Asadullah Kohistani, who did not learn of the Americans' departure until more than two hours after they had left. "We [heard] some rumor that the Americans had left Bagram . . . and finally by seven o'clock in the morning, we understood that it was confirmed that they had already left Bagram," Kohistani said.[19] If ever there was indication that the American commander-in-chief had no plan to evacuate Afghanistan, this was it.

As a result of this callous and irresponsible decision, bordering on the suicidal, the thousands of imprisoned Bagram terrorists were set free to resume their war against America and the West. As an added gift, they and their sponsors were also given an arsenal of weapons stockpiled at Bagram to accomplish their sinister and deadly goals. Weapons worth billions of dollars were abandoned along with the base, and delivered into enemy hands. This weaponry included 600,000 state-of-the-art assault rifles, 2,000 armored vehicles, and forty aircraft including advanced Black Hawk helicopters.[20] The watchdog group Open the Books places the totals at 75,000 military vehicles, 600,000 weapons, and 208 airplanes abandoned by U.S. forces in all of Afghanistan.[21]

Not a single American general resigned in protest over this disgrace, which raised the question of whether China, which had an indisputable hammer over Biden and was the chief beneficiary of America's defeat, was making these decisions rather than Biden himself.

No military leader apologized for the disaster. Instead, the military brass took part in the administration's attempt at face-saving addresses to the public, in which evasive answers and incomplete presentations of the facts made them participants in a coverup of the greatest national scandal and gravest defeat of American forces since Pearl Harbor.

The abandonment of Bagram had dire consequences not only for Afghanistan and the war on terror. It had consequences beyond the sheer number of weapons that had been delivered into enemy hands. One of America's crucial advantages vis-à-vis both terrorists and adversarial powers such as China and Iran was its technological edge. Night vision goggles, for example, allowed American-backed forces in Afghanistan to see after dark while the enemy could not. "We own the night" became an expression of confidence and pride among American and Afghan soldiers.

Over the years, the United States had given 16,000 pairs of night vision goggles to Afghanistan's government forces. How many of these fell into enemy hands as a result of the surrender of Bagram is unknown, but even one would reveal the secrets of its construction. This underscores the potential disaster of letting technologically advanced weapons like the goggles and the Black Hawk helicopters pass into enemy hands.

Once Kabul fell, the Biden administration prostrated itself before the Taliban, allowing it to provide security for the chaotic crowds of desperate Afghans and Americans seeking to board flights out of the country. The Biden administration treated the Taliban terrorists like a legitimate government as it partnered with them in security matters. Incredibly, the Biden State Department even provided the Taliban with lists of Afghans who had aided Americans. They did this while the Taliban was going door to door killing people suspected of collaborating with the Americans.[22] While Biden was partnering with the Taliban, the Taliban was beheading an entire family in front of their father, who was then himself beheaded for running afoul of the new rulers in Kabul. And there were many more such murders out of sight.

On August 26, two ISIS suicide bombers were allowed by the Talban security to pass through their check points at the airport and blow themselves up, killing thirteen American troops and 160 Afghans.[23] It was the greatest loss of American soldiers in ten years.[24]

The Afghanistan surrender without a fight was a national humiliation, the worst in American history, wiping out an American image of competence and power that would be difficult to restore, and certainly not possible with a weak, disoriented, inept, and corrupt leader like Joe Biden. His imbecilic decisions (as former British prime minister Tony Blair called the steps that led to the Afghanistan disaster) had a familiar aura. It was as though Biden had made his decisions in a fit of absent-mindedness, which was the same impression made by his thoughtless decision to blow up America's southern border in the midst of a global pandemic and an international war on terror—the reason America was in Afghanistan in the first place.

The spectacle of American incompetence and inhumanity that Biden had created in Afghanistan horrified the American people, who were powerless to stop it or effect a change of course. While some Republicans called for Biden's impeachment as he bowed to the Taliban authority and turned a twenty-year victory into a total defeat, no Democrats did.

While Afghanistan was falling and Islamic barbarism was ascending, and hundreds of thousands of Afghans were facing brutal retribution, the Democrats, led by Nancy Pelosi and Bernie Sanders, were meeting late into the night in the Capitol putting the finishing touches on their $3.5 trillion infrastructure bill—more accurately described as a socialist wish list bill—which no Republican supported.

As for Afghanistan, Pelosi's attitude was "I'm all right Jack," that everything is fine. When asked by CBS if the United States should have sent in more troops to secure the evacuation, she answered: "Well, first may I just say that I commend the president for the action that he took. It was strong, it was decisive, and it was the right thing to do."[25] It was typical of Pelosi's history of lies. Her whole approach added up to an appalling case of misplaced priorities, cold-hearted dishonesty, and callous disregard for the suffering Biden's policies were causing, as well as indifference to the nation's vital interests.

Only Democrats at the Capitol had the means to change course, and every one of them was resolved not to do that. No one in the chain of command resigned. No one spoke up. It was an appalling impasse and depressing statement. From the beginning, America had the power in Afghanistan to command the situation, but the Biden Democrats lacked the will to do so.

How did America's generals allow this travesty—this devastating blow to America's national security—to take place? Where was their attention focused as the exit date for American troops approached?

In February 2021, the May 1 deadline was just two months away, and the Taliban offensive was already in progress. But Biden's Secretary of Defense, General Lloyd Austin, was not ordering a general alert to prepare for the situation in Afghanistan. Instead, he was ordering a two-month stand-down of the military so that military assets could focus on combating existential threats to the American homeland from Trump supporters.[26]

These existential threats did not include the Taliban's campaign to take control of Afghanistan and make it a base of international Islamic terrorism. Instead, the existential threats that concerned the Secretary of Defense and the Joint Chiefs were the threats that had allegedly manifested themselves in the January 6 so-called insurrection at the Capitol: "white supremacy" and "domestic terrorism" from the political right. Both of these threats, like the one that prompted the unprecedented mobilization of 25,000 troops to guard the Capitol, were politically inspired fictions designed to demonize Republicans and advance the radical, economy–busting agendas of the Democrat Party. It was on Democrat orders that 25,000 troops had been mobilized to surround the Capitol and stay there for months at a cost of half a billion dollars, although no domestic terrorists bothered to show up.[27] The 25,000 troops around the Capitol, moreover, was three times the number of American troops in Afghanistan at the time.

The connection to the January 6 event was made clear by Pentagon spokesman Admiral John Kirby, who "noted that some of the extremists who stormed the U.S. Capitol on January 6 were active duty service members and others were military veterans." Secretary Austin admitted "the numbers may be small"—namely double digits—but "they were not as small as anyone would like."[28]

The concern with white supremacy fantasies and right-wing extremism continued after the sixty-day stand-down. On June 24, eight days before the abandonment of the Bagram Air Base to the terrorists, General Milley was defending Critical Race Theory to the House Armed Services Committee, and telling them: "I want to understand white rage," which in Milley's view constituted an internal threat to the armed forces and the nation.[29]

In accord with the anti-Trump hysteria whipped up by the Speaker of the House, the Biden administration had called on the Justice Department, the Department of Homeland Security, and the military to root out the conservative "extremists" in their organizations and to track down and arrest the protesters who hadn't already been arrested on January 6. It was this domestic threat from alleged subversive opponents—and not defending America from its foreign enemies—that inevitably became the focus of Pentagon concerns.

If Milley had said that he wanted to understand the "Taliban rage" or "Muslim rage" that was about to take down a country he was supposed to defend, and if Austin had directed the troops to focus on that problem instead of the forty-odd patriotic servicemen who may have thought the presidential election was stolen, perhaps there might have been objections to the abandonment of Bagram and the withdrawal might have turned out differently. But then Democrat leaders like Nancy Pelosi and Alexandria Ocasio-Cortez might have called Milley's statement "Islamophobic"—which Pelosi had said was one of the three "root causes" of the January 6 protest, and Milley's job would have been in jeopardy.[30] With these political concerns as pressing priorities for the military brass, it is not too difficult to guess how they lost their focus on real threats like al-Qaeda, ISIS, and the Taliban.

10

The November Rejection

RADICAL UTOPIANS SEEKING to change the world invariably have three traits in common. These flow from the radical nature of their mission, which is to change the world. First, radicals are in a hurry. Their task is large and the opportunities to achieve it scarce. America's political culture is specifically designed to support incremental reforms, not abrupt breaks with the past. Ramming through transformational changes on the basis of razor thin majorities is exactly what the American system is designed to frustrate and thwart. But this is the very goal of radicals, and they are consequently pitted from the outset against the majority.

Second, because radicals are in a hurry, they are impatient with process and persuasion, which makes them generally tone deaf to the majority that opposes them.

Radicals dismiss their opponents, because once their schemes are implemented—by whatever means necessary—they are confident that a majority will see just how liberating their policies are, and they will be grateful. Blinded by arrogance, they prefer government by mandate and *diktat* to the frustrating conversations that are the life blood of a democratic system.

Third, radicals generate energy for their movements by singling out a social subgroup, usually a racial or religious minority, to demonize as the enemy of these liberating schemes. In this way they remove opponents from the deliberative process and deny them a proverbial "seat at the table" where they can express their opposition.

All these ingrained attitudes among Democrats had built up an opposition to the Biden agendas and sparked a resistance to his policies. Biden's response to this opposition was to dismiss his opponents as "white supremacists" who were making "racist dog whistles" in the direction of their deplorable base. His war against "anti-vaxxers" served a similar purpose. After a year of failed policies, crises at the border and record inflation, Biden had little credibility left and his counter-attacks only generated increased opposition.

Additionally, if he were so inclined, Biden was prevented from attempting a course correction by the fact that Democrats were a deeply divided body. A vocal "progressive caucus" composed of 96 House Members wanted more "transformational" policies, and opposed any retrenchments, or concessions to their critics. When left-wing teacher unions and school boards refused to reopen schools for in-class teaching, the Zoom lessons they provided had the unintended effect of revealing to parents the radicals' well-funded and well-advanced program to indoctrinate their children in anti-American race theories and gender extremism.

Unintended Consequences

Prior to the in-home Zoom courses, few parents were aware of what the "anti-racist" and "equity" indoctrination curricula their children were receiving actually entailed. In official documents earmarked only for teachers and public school administrators, the stated purpose of these "equity" programs was to "engage in the disruption and dismantling of white supremacy and systemic racism," which was alleged to characterize American democracy since its creation.[1] In addition, K-12 students as early as kindergarten were being exposed to radical theories of gender fluidity. Many books being used even in lower grades were sexually explicit, containing scenes of homosexual sex and even bestiality—all justified by leftist teachers and administrators as promoting "inclusion."

As a result, throughout the summer of 2021 parents began flocking to once-sleepy school board meetings, demanding explanations. When school board members denied that any racialized indoctrination was taking place, parents read out loud into the record excerpts from some of the books and handouts being used. "All white people are racist or complicit by virtue of benefiting from privileges that are not something they can voluntarily renounce," one parent read from Barbara Applebaum's book, *Being White, Being Good*.[2]

Far from being directed only at white people, Critical Race Theory is an assault on the very foundations and institutions of American society and the West in general. Robin D'Angelo is the author of *White Fragility*, which may be the most widely used text in diversity training seminars and school classrooms. This sweeping condemnation of white people, America, and western civilization are typical of the radical movement that has infiltrated the schools: "White people raised in Western society are conditioned into a white supremacist worldview because it is the bedrock of our society and its institutions. . . . Entering the conversation with this understanding is freeing because it allows us to focus on how—rather than if—our racism is manifest."

In pushing back on parents protesting this racial and civilizational hatred, school boards in Virginia and elsewhere claimed that the parents were just objecting to "history." But these doctrines constituted an ideological attack rather than a scholarly inquiry, as manifest in this statement by one of the movement's avatars, Harvard lecturer, and editor of the magazine *Race Traitor*, Noel Ignatiev: "We believe that so long as the white race exists, all movements against what is called 'racism' will fail. Therefore, our aim is to abolish the white race."[3]

Far from being an academic inquiry into the past, the Critical Race Theory program was as if Virginia and other school districts had offered contracts to the Chinese Communist Party to provide a curriculum and instructors to teach a Marxist-Leninist history of American imperialism.

Perhaps the "equity" practice that enraged parents most was the separation of children into racial groups with white students being characterized as "oppressors" and all others as their victims. The objections to this racist practice were as vociferous coming from black parents who did not want their children to think of themselves as victims, as they were coming from whites, who didn't want their children being tarred as "racist oppressors" of their non-white classmates.

The Battle Grows

As the school boards continued to stonewall their critics and dismiss them as "white supremacists" who shouldn't be interfering with the educational process, parental protests intensified and school board meetings became more raucous. At a meeting on June 22 of the Loudon County school board, an irate father accused the school superintendent Scott Ziegler of covering up the rape of his daughter in a "gender fluid" bathroom—a feature of the school system's progressive agendas—where she was attacked by a transgender "male" student in a skirt.[4] The school authorities flatly denied that the incident had occurred and transferred the rapist to another school, where he promptly repeated the crime.

Ziegler's response to the father's protest was to claim that "the predator transgender student or person simply does not exist," and that, "we don't have any record of

assaults occurring in our restrooms." But as was later revealed, he and other board members learned of the sexual
assault against the girl on the day it happened.[5] Enraged
by Ziegler's denials, the father became so emotional that
the officials ordered police officers in attendance to remove him. The protesting father resisted and was wres-
tled to the floor.

In the hands of the left-wing teacher unions, this
quickly became an alleged case of parental "violence,"
and was invoked by the left-wing National School Board
Association in a letter appealing to the White House to
bring a heavier hand into the fray.[6]

Documents uncovered under the Freedom of Information Act (FOIA) reveal that the White House had actually worked behind the scenes with teacher unions and
the National School Boards Association to help draft the
six-page letter,[7] which referred to the distraught parents
as "domestic terrorists" and called on the federal government to take action against what it described as the parents' "heinous actions [that] could be the equivalent to a
form of domestic terrorism and hate crimes."[8]

Within five days, the Attorney General of the United
States, Merrick Garland, issued a memorandum directing the FBI and the Justice Department to investigate
what he called "a disturbing spike in harassment, intimidation, and threats of violence against school administrators, board members, teachers, and staff."[9] Sen. Josh
Hawley (R-MO) produced a secret memorandum from
one of Garland's U.S. Attorneys who listed 13 different
federal crimes that unruly parents could be charged with

even for nonviolent acts. Among the federal crimes ambitious prosecutors could use against disobedient parents were "making annoying phone calls" and "using the internet in a way that might cause emotional distress."[10]

Criminalizing parents concerned that their children were getting a mis-education in the public school system was the kind of response one would expect from a police state not a democracy, but it was characteristic of Democrat attitudes toward their critics.

During the congressional hearings to which he was summoned Garland withered under the angry questioning of Republican senators and congressmen who demanded that he resign immediately.[11] During these congressional interrogations, the head of the Department of Justice was forced to admit that he relied solely on the letter from the left-wing school board association when issuing his memorandum, had not conducted any research of his own, and that the "threats of violence" that he claimed justified such unprecedented attacks on the political liberties of parents were virtually nonexistent.

The November Election

Despite these ominous government responses, America was still a democracy, and while these battles were taking place, the Democrats were facing bruising gubernatorial and school board elections across the country. They were particularly desperate to maintain control of one of their greatest prizes, the once solidly Republican Commonwealth of Virginia, which due to a recent influx of new immigrants and government workers had voted for Biden by 10 percentage points in the 2020 election.

As the campaigns got under way, polls showed that former Democrat governor Terry McAuliffe was 9 points ahead of Republican businessman Glenn Youngkin, his rival for the governor's office.[12] But then Youngkin, a complete unknown who had never held public office, began talking about what was happening in Virginia schools. During a candidate debate, he promised that if elected governor he would "ban Critical Race Theory on day one." McAuliffe responded haughtily, "I don't think parents should be telling schools what they should teach."[13]

Polls soon showed Youngkin pulling ahead. The Democrats panicked, and resorted to demonizing their opponents and denouncing school board critics as "white supremacists," insisting first that Critical Race Theory is only taught in law schools and then that it actually didn't exist at all.[14]

Such tactics fooled no one—particularly since many black parents, armed with the actual texts being used in schools, also denounced as un-American the Critical Race Theory-inspired teachings about the evils of "whiteness" and the permanent oppression of all blacks. One black mother told the Loudon School Board that the Critical Race Theory teachings taught in its schools were themselves racist and "a tactic that was used by Hitler and the Ku Klux Klan."[15]

When the votes were counted on November 2, Democrats had lost the governorship and their 55–45 majority in the Virginia House of Delegates, a stunning defeat for their agendas.[16]

Nor was Virginia the only state in which Democrats took an historic beating. They also lost local elections in New Jersey, Connecticut, California, and Texas, where similar battles over the schools and Democrat policies had taken place. In New Jersey, Democrat Party boss and president of the state senate Steve Sweeney, who spent $1 million on his campaign, lost to a truck driver who spent $153.[17] The New Jersey governor, Democrat Phil Murphy, barely won reelection against Republican Jack Ciattarelli.[18]

It was the same in Texas. In San Antonio, Republican John Lujan won a special election in a district that Biden had carried by 14 points.[19] Even in Pennsylvania and Biden's home state of Delaware[20], candidates who campaigned against Critical Race Theory and mask mandates in schools scored huge victories.[21]

More ominously for the Democrats, their *issues* were firmly repudiated by voters. In Seattle, Bruce Harrell, who advocated adding *more* police rather than defunding them, easily defeated leftist city council president Lorena González for mayor. In the race for city attorney, Republican Ann Davison defeated radical police-abolitionist Nicole Thomas-Kennedy by 30 points.[22] The same was true in Minneapolis, like Seattle the scene of violent riots and arson throughout 2020. Voters there resoundingly rejected a measure to replace the Minneapolis Police Department with a "Department of Public Safety."[23]

Democrats in Denial

The Democrats responded to this rejection by the electorate by attributing it to "white supremacy" and the fact that they hadn't been able to pass enough of their trillion-dollar socialist programs. In particular, the "human infrastructure" bill—now called the "Build Back Better" initiative—had been stalled by internal divisions in the party: "People are upset and uncertain about a lot of things," Biden told reporters, "from COVID to school to jobs to a whole range of things and the cost of a gallon of gasoline. And so if I'm able to pass and sign into law my Build Back Better initiative, I'm in a position where you're going to see a lot of things ameliorated, quickly and swiftly."[24] How spending trillions more government dollars would ameliorate the inflation problem, or resolve the conflict over racist instruction in the classroom, or any of the other problems he alluded to, was not obvious to anyone outside the Democrat bubble.

The Democrats' claim that white supremacy was responsible for their defeats was also ludicrous in the face of the facts. Along with Youngkin, Virginia voters had elected a Cuban American as the state's first Hispanic Attorney General, and Marine Corps veteran Winsome Sears, the first black Lieutenant Governor in the history of the Commonwealth. In her acceptance speech, Sears gave the lie not only to the Democrats' Virginia campaign to tar Republicans as racists, but to the Critical Race Theory curriculum that attempted to tar the nation itself as a white supremacist nightmare:

I'm telling you that what you are looking at is the American dream. When my father came to this country, August 11th of 1963, he came at the height of the Civil Rights Movement from Jamaica. He came and I said to him, "But it was such a bad time for us. Why did you come?" And he said, "Because America was where the jobs and the opportunities were."

And he only came with $1.75. *$1.75!* Took any job he could find, and he put himself through school and started his American dream. And now, he's comfortably retired. And then, he came and got me when I was six years old. And when I stepped on that Pan Am Boeing 737 and landed at JFK, I landed in a new world. And so let me tell you this. I am not even first generation American. When I joined the Marine Corps, I was still a Jamaican. But this country had done so much for me, I was willing, willing to die for this country.

.... There are some who want to divide us and we must not let that happen. They would like us to believe we are back in 1963 when my father came. We can live where we want. We can eat where we want. We own the water fountains. We have had a Black president elected, not once, but twice. And here, I am living proof.[25]

Living proof for Americans but not for progressive ideologues. "The problem is here they want White supremacy by ventriloquist effect," explained Democrat commentator Michael Eric Dyson, in a November 4 segment on MSNBC. "There is a Black mouth moving but a

White idea . . . running on the runway of the tongue of a figure who justifies and legitimates the White supremacist practices."[26]

Staying the Course

In sum, in the wake of the rejection of their policies and agendas at the ballot box, Democrats were determined to double down as though the vote hadn't taken place. Like the authoritarians in whose footsteps the Democrats were following, they regarded elections as obstacles rather than opportunities. That would explain their determination to demonize their opponents, to take authority away from the states and centralize the voting system in Washington, to press for universal unsolicited mail-in ballots, and to make their primary political campaign a crusade against voter IDs and election integrity.

"We screw up this voting thing and [Georgia Democrat] Warnock ain't going to be in the Senate and we ain't going to win nothing in North Carolina and we won't have a chance down in Florida," explained presidential kingmaker and Democrat Majority Whip James Clyburn (D-SC), referring to the Democrats' efforts to change the nation's voting laws.[27] Biden won the State of Georgia with fewer than 12,000 voters, yet according to the Democrats themselves, 270,000 voters in Georgia have no ID and were still able to vote in the 2020 election.[28]

Democrats have already codified their plans to centralize elections under Washington control, rely on fraud-friendly unsolicited mail-in ballots, legitimize "ballot harvesting" and "vote navigators," along with other practices that the bipartisan Carter-Baker Commission on Federal Election Reform warned were fraud-facilitating practices in HR-1, the "For the People Act" passed by Nancy Pelosi's House in 2021. Nothing could be clearer than the fact that the Democrat Party is on a mission to dismantle the political system under whose auspices Americans have prospered for more than 240 years. Believing, as so-called progressives, that they are on the "right side of history"—it is not clear what, if anything, would deter them from this destructive path.

11

Where Are We Headed?

IN A TWIST of fate, the anniversary of Trump's "Stop the Steal" rally took place three days after the anniversary of his successful assassination of General Qassim Soleimani, Iran's terrorist leader.[1] The killing of Soleimani eliminated an enemy responsible for thousands of deaths in the Middle East including all the Americans who had been killed by Iranian I.E.Ds in the war in Iraq. Trump's decision to kill the chief terrorist in the Middle East—an historic victory for the United States—was roundly criticized at the time by Biden and the Democrats, who regarded it as improper and provocative.

Iranian leaders, on the other hand, viewed the anniversary of Soleimani's death as an occasion to threaten revenge. Every American intelligence official and Pentagon officer was put on alert.[2] As chairman of the Joint Chiefs,

General Mark Milley was at the center of the meetings concerned with America's response.

National security officials held their regular meeting on January 2, during which they discussed the Iranian threat. The scene was described by *Washington Post* reporters and authors of an anti-Trump book titled *I Alone Can Fix It*:

"Milley and his colleagues conferred about Iran's saber-rattling, including a speech by Iranian president Hassan Rouhani the night before in which he seemed to make a thinly veiled threat on Trump's life. 'Trump . . . will soon be deposed not just from office but from life,' Rouhani said. 'The disappearance of the criminal Trump will bring quiet and stability to the region and throughout the world. He perpetrated many crimes but the economic embargo on Iran and the assassination of [Qassim] Soleimani are crimes we cannot forgive.'"[3]

The threats prompted Trump's chief of staff to call a special meeting at the White House for the next day. Trump returned to Washington from his holiday retreat in Mar-a-Lago to attend the meeting with General Milley, Milley's staff, and other officials. According to the *Post* reporters, Milley's chief concern was not Rouhani but the tweets Trump had made that night complaining about the recent presidential election: "Milley told close aides that listening to the president was like reading George Orwell's *1984*. 'Lies are truth. Division is unity. Evil is good,' the general said, mimicking the dystopian novel."[4]

The Trump tweets that disturbed Milley were calls to his supporters to gather at the Ellipse for the "Stop the Steal" rally four days away. Milley was convinced the

Tweets had a more sinister intent. "Milley told his staff that he believed Trump was stoking unrest, possibly in hopes of an excuse to invoke the Insurrection Act and call out the military."[5]

The *Post* reporters continued their account: "A student of history, Milley saw Trump as the classic authoritarian leader with nothing to lose. He described to aides that he kept having this stomach-churning feeling that some of the worrisome early stages of twentieth-century fascism in Germany were replaying in twenty-first-century America. He saw parallels between Trump's rhetoric of election fraud and Adolf Hitler's insistence to his followers at the Nuremberg rallies that he was both a victim and their savior. 'This is a *Reichstag* moment,' Milley told aides. 'The gospel of the *Führer*.'"[6]

At the same time that the chairman of the Joint Chiefs of Staff was telling national security officials that Trump was Hitler and was probably planning a military coup, he was steadfastly maintaining that his mission was to defend the political neutrality of the military. At the same time, however, he was rallying his Pentagon associates to refuse to cooperate with Trump's alleged treason. In a conversation with his closest deputies regarding a possible Trump coup, Milley said: "They may try, but they're not going to f—king succeed. You can't do this without the military. You can't do this without the CIA and the FBI. We're the guys with the guns."[7]

We're the guys with the guns. It was a perfect refutation of the Democrats' entire case that January 6 was a planned insurrection by Donald Trump.

Eight days later, on January 14, wrote the *Post* reporters, dozens of military and law enforcement leaders gathered at Fort Myer for a drill exercise. They took over a
large gymnasium and mapped out the city on the floor
to imagine where people might congregate, where security forces would be staged, which buildings snipers
would occupy, and which intersections would be accessible.[8] The city they were studying was not Kabul. It was
Washington, D.C.[9]

Milley helped lead the drill and, in an initial smaller
meeting with the more senior national security leaders,
laid out the stakes. "Here's the deal, guys: These guys are
Nazis, they're boogaloo boys, they're Proud Boys. These
are the same people we fought in World War II," Milley
told them. "Everyone in this room, whether you're a cop,
whether you're a soldier, we're going to stop these guys
to make sure we have a peaceful transfer of power. We're
going to put a ring of steel around the Capitol and these
Nazis aren't going to get in."[10]

As conservative Fox anchor Tucker Carlson reminded
his TV audience, Milley was "referring to American citizens. A ring of steel to repel the QAnon shaman and several hundred senior citizens from Orlando with signs.
This is a guy, by the way, who's paid to assess threats
realistically. What countries pose a threat to the United
States? Put them in order. If you think the QAnon shaman is the same as the S.S., maybe you're not so good at
that."[11]

Take a moment to appreciate the spectacle. The head of
a terrorist Islamic dictatorship, which is a mortal enemy

of the United States, with thousands of American deaths on its head, issues a public death sentence against the elected president of the United States. And the chairman of the Joint Chiefs of America's military force brushes it off because he is concerned about a more pressing threat—for which he has no evidence: that an American president, who had just received the votes of 74 million Americans on an "America First" promise, is actually a closet Adolf Hitler, and his followers Nazis.

In Milley's twisted mind, he is keeping the military out of politics, even as he mobilizes national security officials to approach his commander-in-chief as a national security threat, an Adolf Hitler-in-the-making, and possibly planning a military coup. The General's solution? Ring the Capitol with 25,000 troops to face an army of domestic terrorists who never showed up.

That such a confused, ignorant, and fanatical individual is the head America's military forces ought to be deeply troubling to anyone concerned not only about civilian control of the military but the security of America itself. That not one of the military and security figures whom Milley approached to undermine their civilian commander-in-chief stepped forward to protest these treasonous actions should be an equally troubling revelation.

But most disturbing of all should be the fact that America's cultural elites and policy experts, from their perches at *The Washington Post*, *The New Yorker*, *The New York Times*, the cable news media, and the national security think tanks—all influencers of America's political fate—should find nothing awry in Milley's fascistic and delusional actions and sound no warnings as to the threats they posed. On the contrary, for casting Trump as the enemy, and violating the constitutional order in the process, the liberal elites regarded Mark Milley as a hero and a scholar.

"You read what Milley was doing," CNN's Anderson Cooper commented on the *Post* revelations, . . . "which you know is obeying the Constitution. It is standing up to the oath that he and serving members have taken. I mean, *that's what a patriot does*" (emphasis added). Actually not.

CNN's Poppy Harlow also gushed: "You think of General Milley as someone who chooses every word with intention and is a student of history and to use the words he used like 'Nazi' and '*Reichstag*' says a lot. . . ." Harlow didn't explain how calling 74 million Americans Nazi sympathizers for voting for their candidate made Milley a credible 'student of history.'[12]

To Tucker Carlson, the only real question was this: "How was Mark Milley still chairman of the Joint Chiefs of Staff?" It was because his views are the core beliefs of the Democrat Party—the party of the righteous—who are out to change the world, and who for five years have treated Trump and his patriotic followers as white supremacists and neo-Nazis, regardless of skin color.

America is not a nation divided between 74 million supporters of Adolf Hitler and a virtuous rest. Challenging an election result is not plotting a coup. On the other hand, being persuaded that it could be is a pretty certain indicator that should the next free and fair election result in a Democrat victory, the party of the righteous will find ways to make sure it is the last.

As with Afghanistan, empires and states rise and fall while everybody is watching. Although the watchers may be surprised when the actual collapse occurs, with the hindsight provided by the end itself, everybody can see how it fell.

Is America already an empty shell of its greater self, and are its days already numbered? Only a fool would say, with any certainty, no. Barbarian terrorist forces are already at the gates, and inside them, American leaders—both military and civilian—are preoccupied with delusional threats that are said to be existential—climate change, white supremacy, patriotic extremism. But the greatest existential threat to American democracy is the drive by the Democrat Party to create a one-party socialist state—a fascist state. This is manifest in their assault on the First Amendment through so-called "cancel culture" and their collusion in the deplatforming of a president of the United States and his 74 million supporters.

They have pressed for the dismantling of the system of checks and balances, which has been the bulwark of American democracy for over 240 years. They have done this by demonizing their domestic political opponents, attempting to abolish the Electoral College, and pushing to abolish the filibuster and to pack the Supreme Court; they have attacked the integrity of the electoral system by opposing voter IDs; they have assaulted anyone who questions election results as enemies of American democracy; and they have replaced America's liberating culture of individualism with a tribal identity politics that undermines the foundations of the constitutional system.

Finally, while handing Islamic terrorists their greatest victory since 9/11, they have sought to attack and discredit their democratic opponents as "domestic extremists" and terrorists. Their zealous advocacy of socialist economics and political fascism sets us on the path to a totalitarian future. All that awaits the sad conclusion to these efforts are the *gulags* and deprogramming camps, which they are not shy about promoting.

Acknowledgments

I have been blessed as an author by support from many sources: John Perazzo has been my go-to researcher; writer Robert J. Hutchinson is a new friend and the principal contributor to chapter 6 of this volume. My brilliant and talented sons Jon and Ben, and my stepson—also Jon—have provided me with moral support, which seems to be ever more indispensable as the years go by. And Steve Schuck has become my one-man promoter and late life friend. As they have for all my books, my board and staff at the Freedom Center; my good buddy Wally Nunn; my board members, Larry Post, Mallory Danaher, Nina Cunningham, and Marc Shapiro; my lawyer Paul Hoffman; my captain, Mike Finch; and my staffers, Liz Ruiz, Jamie Glazov, Lily Gonzalez, Nelson Ines, and Todd

Snider have all played crucial roles in enabling me to do what I have done.

Finally, I have now written four volumes in defense of our country for Chris Ruddy and the editors at Humanix Books. I hope my countrymen and countrywomen are as grateful for their assistance in making these books possible as I am.

Endnotes

PRELUDE

1. https://www.c-span.org/video/?477598-1/president-trump
   -holds-rally-butler-pennsylvania
2. Michael C. Bender, *Frankly, We Did Win This Election: The Inside
   Story of How Trump Lost*, Kindle Edition, location 5804
3. https://www.foxnews.com/politics/trump-speech-at-michigan
   -rally-interrupted-by-we-love-you-chant
4. Bender, op. cit., loc 5902
5. Bender, op. cit., loc 5976
6. Bender op. cit., loc 6042

CHAPTER 1

1. https://www.heritage.org/conservatism/commentary/preventing
   -the-tyranny-the-majority
2. David Horowitz, *The Great Betrayal: The Black Book of the American
   Left*, vol III, Second Thoughts Books, 2013
3. https://www.dailysignal.com/2020/11/20/7-ways-the-2005-carter
   -baker-report-could-have-averted-problems-with-2020-election

4. https://thefederalist.com/2020/12/03/were-insecure-voting-processes-this-years-insurance-policy-for-democrats

5. https://www.discoverthenetworks.org/organizations/the-2020-presidential-election-fraud; https://thehill.com/homenews/campaign/469948-democrats-challenge-election-laws-in-; https://www.reuters.com/article/uk-usa-election-biden-idUKKBN24305J

6. https://www.heritage.org/election-integrity/commentary/the-risks-mail-voting; https://www.washingtonexaminer.com/news/trump-suggests-the-delaying-the-election-until-americans-can-vote-securely

7. https://www.washingtonexaminer.com/news/trump-suggests-the-delaying-the-election-until-americans-can-vote-securely

8. https://www.axios.com/poll-democrats-and-republicans-hate-each-other-racist-ignorant-evil-99ae7afc-5a51-42be-8ee2-3959e43ce320.html

9. https://www.facebook.com/101155774697123/posts/pennsylvania-supreme-court-with-a-5-2-democrat-majority-overrules-judge-that-sta/217868189692547

10. https://www.theblaze.com/op-ed/levin-on-january-6-we-learn-whether-our-constitution-will-hold

11. https://www.lincolninstitute.org/pennsylvania-bombshell-biden-99-4-vs-trump-0-6

12. https://bannonswarroom.com/wp-content/uploads/2020/12/The-Immaculate-Deception-12.15.20-1.pdf

13. https://www.businessinsider.com/trump-campaign-lawsuits-election-results-2020-11

14. https://bannonswarroom.com/wp-content/uploads/2020/12/The-Immaculate-Deception-12.15.20-1.pdf

15. https://bannonswarroom.com/wp-content/uploads/2020/12/The-Immaculate-Deception-12.15.20-1.pdf (p. 2)

16. https://www.usatoday.com/story/news/politics/elections/2020/10/23/debate-transcript-trump-biden-final-presidential-debate-nashville/3740152001

17. https://ballotpedia.org/Presidential_election,_2020

18. https://ballotpedia.org/Presidential_election,_2020

19. https://www.reuters.com/article/usa-election-trump/trump-vows-to-intervene-in-texas-election-case-before-supreme-court-idUSKBN28J1VJ

20. https://twitter.com/realDonaldTrump/status /1337620892139081728?s=20

21. https://www.nbcnews.com/politics/supreme-court/supreme -court-rejects-texas-effort-overturn-election-fatal-blow -trump-n1250883

22. Senator Jeanne Shaheen of New Hampshire, for instance, asserted that Republicans who were questioning Biden's victory "are bordering on sedition and treason." https://www.foxnews .com/politics/democratic-senator-some-gop-members-bordering -sedition-treason

23. https://www.washingtonpost.com/politics/trump-uses-power-of -presidency-to-try-to-overturn-the-election-and-stay-in-office /2020/11/19/bc89caa6-2a9f-11eb-8fa2-06e7cbb145c0_story.html

24. https://www.washingtonpost.com/opinions/2021/01/06 /president-trump-has-committed-treason

25. https://thepostmillennial.com/watch-trump-offered-national -guard-capitol-denied; Calvin Freiburger, "DC Mayor Refused Trump's Offers of National Guard Aid, Former WH Chief of Staff Says," Lifesitenews.com, February 10, 2021 https://www .lifesitenews.com/news/dc-mayor-refused-trumps-offers-of -national-guard-aid-meadows-says; Prakash Gogoi, "Trump's Offer of 10,000 Troops for Jan. 6 Was Refused," VisionTimes .com, February 13, 2021, https://visiontimes.com/2021/02/13 /trumps-offer-of-10000-troops-for-jan-6-was-declined.html; "Trump Offered 10,000 Troops to Protect DC on January 6th," Zone News, February 2021, https://zonenews-24.com/2021/02 /11/trump-offered-10000-troops-to-protect-dc-on-january-6th

26. https://thepostmillennial.com/watch-trump-offered-national -guard-capitol-denied

27. https://www.npr.org/2021/02/10/966396848/read-trumps-jan-6 -speech-a-key-part-of-impeachment-trial

CHAPTER 2

1. https://www.npr.org/2021/02/09/965472049/the-capitol-siege -the-arrested-and-their-stories; https://www.businessinsider.in /international/news/most-of-the-arrests-from-the-capitol-riots -have-been-misdemeanor-curfew-violations-this-searchable-table -shows-everyone-charged-so-far-/articleshow/80193894.cms

2. https://www.newsweek.com/mary-trump-republicans-capitol
   -riots-traitors-1607406
3. https://www.npr.org/2021/02/09/965472049/the-capitol-siege
   -the-arrested-and-their-stories
4. https://www.npr.org/2021/02/09/965472049/the-capitol-siege
   -the-arrested-and-their-stories
5. Ibid.
6. https://www.npr.org/2021/02/09/965472049/the-capitol-siege
   -the-arrested-and-their-stories
7. https://www.reuters.com/world/us/exclusive-fbi-finds-scant
   -evidence-us-capitol-attack-was-coordinated-sources-2021-08-20
8. https://www.reuters.com/world/us/exclusive-fbi-finds-scant
   -evidence-us-capitol-attack-was-coordinated-sources-2021-08-20
9. https://www.reuters.com/world/us/exclusive-fbi-finds-scant
   -evidence-us-capitol-attack-was-coordinated-sources-2021-08-20
10. https://www.npr.org/2021/02/09/965472049/the-capitol-siege
    -the-arrested-and-their-stories
11. https://www.npr.org/2021/02/09/965472049/the-capitol-siege
    -the-arrested-and-their-stories; https://archive.fo/7A2Bp#selection
    -1427.0-1427.25; https://www.youtube.com/watch?v=MYV
    _Gn0oZ0c&t=186s; https://www.politico.com/f/?id=00000178
    -7031-dae3-affa-f6f7374a0000#page=6
12. https://www.revolver.news/2021/06/stewart-rhodes-oath
    -keepers-missing-link-fbi-unindicted-co-conspirator
13. https://www.npr.org/2021/02/09/965472049/the-capitol-siege
    -the-arrested-and-their-stories
14. https://www.msn.com/en-us/news/us/tucker-carlson-s-wild
    -baseless-theory-blaming-the-fbi-for-organizing-the-jan-6-capitol
    -riot/ar-AAL74wT
15. https://www.buzzfeednews.com/article/jessicagarrison
    /fbi-informants-in-michigan-kidnap-plot
16. https://www.revolver.news/2021/06/stewart-rhodes-oath
    -keepers-missing-link-fbi-unindicted-co-conspirator
17. https://www.nytimes.com/2021/07/09/us/politics/stewart
    -rhodes-oath-keepers-fbi.html
18. Paul Blest, "The Oath Keepers Started Training to Raid the
    Capitol in November, Prosecutors Say," Vice News, January 28,

2021, https://www.vice.com/en/article/7k9m49/alleged-militia
-members-started-planning-capitol-riot-days-after-bidens-win

19. https://www.cnn.com/2021/03/09/politics/oath-keepers-capitol
-riot-justice-department/index.html

20. https://www.rev.com/blog/transcripts/nancy-pelosi-press
-conference-on-capitol-riot-25th-amendment-transcript
-january-7

21. https://www.rev.com/blog/transcripts/nancy-pelosi-press
-conference-on-capitol-riot-25th-amendment-transcript
-january-7

22. https://www.cnn.com/2021/02/17/politics/capitol-insurrection
-weapons-ron-johnson/index.html)

23. Nexstar Media Wire, "What We Know about the 5 People Who
Died During Riot at U.S. Capitol," KTLA.com, January 8, 2021,
https://ktla.com/news/nationworld/what-we-know-about-the-5
-people-who-died-during-riot-at-u-s-capitol

24. https://www.washingtonexaminer.com/news/new-york-times
-capitol-police-officer-brian-sicknick-fire-extinguisher

25. https://www.nbcnews.com/politics/politics-news/capitol-police
-officer-who-shot-ashli-babbitt-exonerated-internal-probe
-n1277336

26. https://www.politico.com/news/2021/03/29/capitol-police-jan6
-footage-478439

27. https://nypost.com/2021/02/04/aoc-blasted-for-exaggerating
-capitol-riot-experience

28. https://redstate.com/nick-arama/2021/02/03/321029-n321029

29. https://twitter.com/coribush/status
/1348373914481795073?lang=en

30. https://www.rollingstone.com/politics/politics-news/pelosi
-house-select-committee-insurrection-1188874

31. Jon Brown, "'Infamy': Chuck Schumer Compares Capitol Chaos
to Pearl Harbor," *The Daily Wire*, January 6, 2021, https://www
.dailywire.com/news/infamy-chuck-schumer-compares-capitol
-chaos-to-pearl-harbor; "NY Senator Responds to Outrage, Says
Capitol Siege Tweet Evoking 9/11 'an Emotional Response,'"
Radio.Com (1010WINS), January 10, 2021, https://www.radio
.com/1010wins/news/local/outrage-over-ny-senators-tweet

-comparing-9-11-capitol-riot; "Pelosi Announces Independent 9/11-Style Commission on Deadly Capitol Riot," CNBC, February 15, 2021, https://www.cnbc.com/2021/02/15 /bipartisan-support-grows-for-9/11-style-inquiry-into-deadly -capitol-riot.html; Zack Budryk, "Schwarzenegger Compares Capitol Riot to Kristallnacht," *The Hill*, January 10, 2021, https:// thehill.com/blogs/in-the-know/in-the-know/533556 -schwarzenegger-compares-capitol-riot-to-kristallnacht

32. https://www.youtube.com/watch?v=lvyrvaQkl7s

33. https://www.foxnews.com/politics/us-spends-480m-for-troop -deployment-in-dc-after-riot-at-capitol-report https://www .usatoday.com/story/news/politics/elections/2021/03/15/capitol -riots-parts-campus-fence-come-down-razor-wire-removed /4700471001

34. https://www.wsj.com/articles/national-guard-troops-to-end -mission-at-u-s-capitol-11621892027; https://www.militarytimes .com/news/your-military/2021/02/05/national-guard -deployment-to-secure-dc-will-cost-nearly-500-million; https:// www.reuters.com/world/us/national-guard-troops-expect -leave-us-capitol-next-week-officials-2021-05-19; https://www .wsj.com/articles/national-guard-troops-to-end-mission-at-u-s -capitol-11621892027

35. https://www.business-standard.com/article/international /attackers-of-capitol-were-domestic-terrorists-sent-by-trump -nancy-pelosi-121011400055_1.html; https://www.washingtonpost .com/politics/police-capitol-riot-extremists/2021/01/24 /16fdb2bc-5a7b-11eb-b8bd-ee36b1cd18bf_story.html; https:// www.usatoday.com/in-depth/news/politics/elections/2021/03 /21/police-charged-capitol-riot-reignite-concerns-racism -extremism/4738348001

36. https://twitchy.com/brettt-3136/2021/05/12/attorney-general -merrick-garland-testifies-that-white-supremacists-are-our -greatest-domestic-security-threat

37. https://www.militarytimes.com/news/your-military/2021/02/21 /extremism-in-the-ranks-is-a-threat-but-the-pentagons-not-sure -how-to-address-it

38. https://www.reuters.com/world/us/exclusive-fbi-finds-scant
-evidence-us-capitol-attack-was-coordinated-sources-2021-08-20;
https://www.fbi.gov/news/testimony/examining-the-january-6
-attack-on-the-us-capitol-wray-061521

39. https://www.npr.org/2021/02/09/965472049/the-capitol-siege
-the-arrested-and-their-stories

40. https://www.tabletmag.com/sections/news/articles/lee-smith
-insurrectionists-january-6

41. https://www.nationalreview.com/news/mccarthy-calls-on-fbi-to
-brief-intel-committee-on-swalwells-ties-to-alleged-chinese-spy;
https://thehill.com/policy/international/china/529215-swalwell
-california-politicians-targeted-by-chinese-spy-report

42. https://www.foxnews.com/politics/swalwell-compares-trump-to
-usama-bin-laden-he-was-responsible

43. https://www.breitbart.com/politics/2021/02/10/iimpeachment
-democrats-outraged-over-donald-trumps-fight-like-hell-rhetoric
-used-same-slogan

44. https://www.the-sun.com/news/1520376/black-lives-matter-bail
-criminals-kamala-harris

45. https://www.speaker.gov/newsroom/121120-1

46. https://www.speaker.gov/newsroom/121120-1

47. Jamie Raskin, "Speech on Why Senate Should Convict Trump
Transcript: Trump's Second Impeachment Trial," Rev, February
10, 2021
www.rev.com/blog/transcripts/rep-jamie-raskin-speech-on-why
-senate-should-convict-trump-transcript-trumps-second
-impeachment-trial

48. https://www.newsweek.com/ted-lieu-republicans-big-lie-security
-threat-capitol-1574238; https://news.yahoo.com/schumer-slams
-trump-calling-him-202824061.html

49. https://truthout.org/articles/resolution-to-expel-house-gop-who
-voted-to-overturn-election-is-gaining-momentum

50. https://twitter.com/CoriBush/status/1347566317168164865?s=20

51. https://www.discoverthenetworks.org/individuals/jamie-raskin;
https://archive.thinkprogress.org/why-you-have-nothing
-to-fear-from-non-citizen-voting-302eeb43d1cd; http://www

.thesocialcontract.com/artman2/publish/tsc_23_1/tsc_23_1
_horowitz.shtml

52. https://lee.house.gov/news/press-releases/congresswoman-lee
-on-voter-disenfranchisement-and-the-challenge-of-electoral-votes
53. https://ballotpedia.org/Impeachment_of_Donald_Trump,_2021
54. https://thehill.com/homenews/senate/536364-kaine-eyes-next
-week-to-file-trump-censure-aiming-to-bar-him-from-future
55. https://www.washingtontimes.com/news/2021/feb/18/
democrats-bill-would-ban-trumps-name-us-buildings-/
56. https://www.washingtontimes.com/news/2021/feb/18/
democrats-bill-would-ban-trumps-name-us-buildings-/
57. https://www.forbes.com/sites/lisettevoytko/2019/10/23/heres
-every-trump-property-thats-dropped-his-name/?sh=7d8292ba3571
58. https://nypost.com/2021/01/15/aoc-proposes-funding-to
-deprogram-white-supremacists
59. https://www.washingtonexaminer.com/news/aoc-trump-white
-supremacy-work-to-do
60. https://nypost.com/2021/01/15/aoc-proposes-funding-to
-deprogram-white-supremacists
61. Ibid.
62. https://thehill.com/homenews/house/534045-ocasio-cortez
-congress-looking-into-ways-to-rein-in-disinformation
63. https://247sports.com/college/oklahoma-state/Board/103593
/Contents/Cal-Democrat-wants-to-re-education-for-
conservatives—155033048
64. https://thefederalist.com/2021/01/12/nikole-hannah-jones-calls
-for-consequences-deprogramming-for-republicans
65. https://www.politifact.com/factchecks/2020/dec/08/roy-blunt
/blunts-wrong-trump-did-not-get-highest-minority-vo
66. https://www.wsj.com/articles/biden-says-mob-that-stormed
-capitol-were-domestic-terrorists-11610046962
67. The source for the riots figure is the Armed Conflict Location
and Event Data Project (ACLEDP), https://acleddata.com/data
-export-tool; https://thefederalist.com/2020/09/16/study-up-to
-95-percent-of-2020-u-s-riots-are-linked-to-black-lives-matter
68. https://www.discoverthenetworks.org/organizations/blms-close
-ties-to-the-democratic-party

69. https://www.frontpagemag.com/fpm/2021/09/black-lives
    -matter-killed-2000-black-people-daniel-greenfield
70. https://www.foxnews.com/politics/biden-antifa-idea-what-we
    -know
71. https://www.haaretz.com/us-news/pelosi-blasts-trump-and-his
    -stormtroopers-as-portland-s-mayor-tells-troops-to-get-1.9004427
72. https://www.the-sun.com/news/1520376/black-lives-matter-bail
    -criminals-kamala-harris
73. https://thehill.com/homenews/senate/539885-garland-pledges
    -to-prioritize-domestic-terrorism-battle
74. https://www.defenseone.com/threats/2021/05/dhs-doj-look
    -spend-big-countering-violent-domestic-extremism/174002
75. https://www.koin.com/news/protests/riot-declared-as-federal
    -courthouse-attacked-in-portland-070402020; https://
    komonews.com/news/local/photos-protests-rage-in-seattle-over
    -george-floyd-death?photo=1
76. https://factcheck.thedispatch.com/p/did-merrick-garland-say
    -antifa-attacks
77. https://factcheck.thedispatch.com/p/did-merrick-garland-say
    -antifa-attacks
78. https://www.realclearpolitics.com/video/2018/10/04/sen
    _merkley_crew_of_white_republican_men_treat_women_as_if
    _they_are_the_problem.html?spot_im_scroll_to_comments=true
79. https://www.npr.org/2021/02/09/965472049/the-capitol-siege
    -the-arrested-and-their-stories

CHAPTER 3

1. https://www.cnn.com/2021/01/20/politics/joe-biden-speech
   -transcript/index.html
2. https://www.newsweek.com/joe-biden-says-hed-most-progressive
   -president-history-tells-bernie-sanders-disown-1487567
3. https://www.businessinsider.com/us-will-pay-who-200-million
   -reversing-trump-withdrawal-blinken-2021-2; https://www.kff.org
   /coronavirus-covid-19/fact-sheet/the-u-s-government-and-the
   -world-health-organization
4. https://abcnews.go.com/Politics/disaster-motion-34-million
   -travelers-poured-us-coronavirus/story?id=69933625

5. https://www.bbc.com/news/world-middle-east-56665199

6. https://myislam.dk/articles/en/horowitz%20why-israel-is-the
   -victim.php

7. https://www.whitehouse.gov/briefing-room/presidential
   -actions/2021/01/20/executive-order-advancing-racial-equity
   -and-support-for-underserved-communities-through-the-federal
   -government

8. https://www.discoverthenetworks.org/organizations/1776
   -commission

9. https://www.heritage.org/american-founders/impact/new
   -york-times-quietly-edits-1619-project-after-conservative
   -pushback

10. https://www.theatlantic.com/ideas/archive/2019/12/historians
    -clash-1619-project/604093

11. https://chicago.suntimes.com/columnists/2021/1/26/22251548
    /joe-biden-susan-rice-executive-orders-systemic-racism-trump
    -1776-commission-private-prisons-aapi

12. https://www.edweek.org/teaching-learning/biden-administration
    -cites-1619-project-as-inspiration-in-history-grant-proposal/2021
    /04 (April 19, 2021); https://www.federalregister.gov/documents
    /2021/04/19/2021-08068/proposed-priorities-american-history
    -and-civics-education#print

13. https://dailycaller.com/2020/07/16/nyt-writer-nikole-hannah
    -jones-white-people-barbaric-devils

14. https://historynewsnetwork.org/article/174140

15. https://www.politico.com/news/magazine/2020/03/06/1619
    -project-new-york-times-mistake-122248

16. https://www.washingtonexaminer.com/opinion/seven-months
    -later-1619-project-leader-admits-she-got-it-wrong

17. http://www.lib.rochester.edu/IN/RBSCP/Frederick_Douglass
    /ATTACHMENTS/Douglass_Fifth_of_July_Speech.pdf

18. However, the Constitution does address slavery—in Article I,
    Section 9, Clause 1, which "prohibited the federal government
    from limiting the importation of persons."

19. https://www.whitehouse.gov/briefing-room/speeches-remarks
    /2021/01/26/remarks-by-president-biden-at-signing-of-an
    -executive-order-on-racial-equity

20. https://www.whitehouse.gov/briefing-room/speeches-remarks
/2021/01/26/remarks-by-president-biden-at-signing-of-an
-executive-order-on-racial-equity

21. https://www.facebook.com/POTUS/posts/the-fact-is-systemic
-racism-touches-every-facet-of-american-life-and-everyone-no
/113716850704852

22. https://www.census.gov/library/stories/2020/09/poverty-rates
-for-blacks-and-hispanics-reached-historic-lows-in-2019.html

23. https://en.wikipedia.org/wiki/List_of_ethnic_groups_in_the
_United_States_by_household_income

24. https://www.whitehouse.gov/briefing-room/presidential-actions
/2021/01/20/executive-order-advancing-racial-equity-and
-support-for-underserved-communities-through-the-federal
-government

25. Ibid.

26. https://www.frontpagemag.com/fpm/2021/06/bidens-racist
-farm-reparations-matthew-vadum
https://townhall.com/tipsheet/leahbarkoukis/2021/07/09
/judge-blocks-biden-administrations-racist-farm-relief-plan
-n2592277

27. https://katv.com/news/nation-world/biden-faces-backlash-over
-vow-to-prioritize-minority-owned-businesses

CHAPTER 4

1. https://www.nytimes.com/2021/07/28/opinion/noncitizen
-voting-us-elections.html

2. https://cis.org/Arthur/Words-Alien-and-Assimilation-Banned
-Biden-administration

3. https://www.cnn.com/2014/11/20/politics/republican-response
-obama-immigration-speech/index.html

4. https://obamawhitehouse.archives.gov/realitycheck/the-press
-office/2011/03/28/remarks-president-univision-town-hall

5. https://www.texastribune.org/2011/07/25/obama-on
-immigration-reform-blame-republicans

6. https://townhall.com/tipsheet/katiepavlich/2014/11/19/jon
-karl-does-obama-think-hes-emperor-of-the-united-states
-n1920606

7. Stanley Kurtz: *Radical-in-Chief,* Threshold Books, 2010; David Horowitz, *Barack Obama's Rules for Revolution,* 2009

8. https://www.uscis.gov/humanitarian/consideration-of-deferred -action-for-childhood-arrivals-daca

9. https://www.uscis.gov/archive/2014-executive-actions-on -immigration

10. https://www.youtube.com/watch?v=1e_7hZOdsxo

11. https://www.cbp.gov/newsroom/stats/sw-border-migration -fy2020

12. https://cis.org/Mortensen/President-Trumps-Executive-Order -Puts-Americans-First-Least-75-Illegal-Aliens-Eligible; https:// www.govinfo.gov/content/pkg/FR-2017-01-30/pdf/2017-02102.pdf; https://www.whitehouse.gov/briefing-room/presidential -actions/2021/02/02/executive-order-creating-a-comprehensive -regional-framework-to-address-the-causes-of-migration-to -manage-migration-throughout-north-and-central-america-and -to-provide-safe-and-orderly-processing; https://www.newsmax .com/politics/asylum/2021/02/12/id/1009873

13. https://cis.org/Report/Bidens-Executive-Actions-President -Unilaterally-Changes-Immigration-Policy

14. https://cis.org/Mortensen/President-Trumps-Executive-Order -Puts-Americans-First-Least-75-Illegal-Aliens-Eligible; https:// www.govinfo.gov/content/pkg/FR-2017-01-30/pdf/2017-02102 .pdf

15. https://www.whitehouse.gov/briefing-room/presidential-actions /2021/02/02/executive-order-creating-a-comprehensive-regional -framework-to-address-the-causes-of-migration-to-manage -migration-throughout-north-and-central-america-and-to -provide-safe-and-orderly-processing; https://www.newsmax .com/politics/asylum/2021/02/12/id/1009873

16. https://dailycaller.com/2021/04/27/biden-94-immigration -orders-first-100-days

17. https://www.foxnews.com/opinion/biden-immigration-order -hide-crimes-victims-hans-von-spakovsky-ken-cuccinelli

18. https://www.attorneysnewshubb.com/2021/06/12/biden-admin -dismantles-voice-trump-office-for-reporting-crimes-by -immigrants

19. https://www.cato.org/publications/immigration-research-policy
    -brief/criminal-immigrants-2017-their-numbers-demographics
    #incarcerations
20. https://www.govinfo.gov/content/pkg/CREC-2016-03-16/html
    /CREC-2016-03-16-pt1-PgE324-3.htm
21. https://immigration.procon.org/questions/does-illegal
    -immigration-relate-to-higher-crime-incidence/#quote-1275
22. https://thehill.com/opinion/immigration/407312-one-in-five-us
    -prison-inmates-is-a-criminal-alien
23. https://www.fairus.org/issue/publications-resources/biden
    -immigration-bill-something-everyone-except-american-public
24. Ibid.
25. https://www.dailymail.co.uk/news/article-9277299/Trump
    -immigration-architect-Stephen-Miller-SLAMS-radical-Biden
    -plan-radical-written.html
26. https://www.washingtonpost.com/immigration/border-arrests
    -surge-cctober-trump/2020/11/19/4155cf7a-2ab2-11eb-b847
    -66c66ace1afb_story.html
27. https://nypost.com/2021/06/13/bidens-illegal-immigration
    -welcome-mat-caused-border-crisis; https://www.usatoday.com
    /story/news/politics/2021/08/12/migrant-encounters-southern
    -border-topped-200-k-july-cbp-says/8113459002; https://www
    .dailywire.com/news/breaking-biden-border-crisis-sinks-to-worst
    -level-in-dhs-history-explodes-674-over-last-year; https://www
    .foxnews.com/politics/migrant-southern-border-june-topping
    -1m-fiscal-year
28. https://www.dailywire.com/news/breaking-biden-border-crisis
    -sinks-to-worst-level-in-dhs-history-explodes-674-over-last-year
29. https://nypost.com/2021/08/03/over-19k-unaccompanied
    -children-stopped-at-border-in-july-report
30. https://cis.org/Arthur/Inadmissible-Aliens-Southwest-Border
    -Ports-Jump-30-Percent-June
31. https://www.theepochtimes.com/mkt_morningbrief/border
    -patrol-apprehends-172000-illegal-immigrants-in-march
    _3767958.html
32. https://www.justice.gov/opa/pr/attorney-general-announces
    -zero-tolerance-policy-criminal-illegal-entry; https://www

.nytimes.com/2018/06/20/us/politics/family-separation
-executive-order.html

33. https://www.cnn.com/2019/06/18/politics/alexandria-ocasio
-cortez-concentration-camps-migrants-detention/index.html;
https://insidesources.com/n-h-dems-call-ice-employees-gestapo
-claim-theyre-running-childrens-concentration-camps

34. https://www.facebook.com/watch/?v=687114181930327

35. https://www.commondreams.org/news/2018/06/07/unethical
-ineffective-and-inhumane-democrats-demand-end-trumps
-family-separation; https://thehill.com/homenews/news/398167
-biden-rips-trump-immigration-policy-one-of-the-darkest
-moments-in-our-history; https://thehill.com/blogs/blog-briefing
-room/news/394434-bernie-sanders-calls-for-trumps-disastrous
-immigration-policy; https://www.cnn.com/2018/06/30/politics
/elizabeth-warren-ice-immigration-protests/index.html

36. https://www.businessinsider.com/migrant-children-in-cages
-2014-photos-explained-2018-5?op=1

37. https://www.nbcnews.com/politics/immigration/trump-says-he
-ll-sign-order-stopping-separation-families-border-n885061

38. https://www.usatoday.com/story/news/factcheck/2020/08/26
/fact-check-obama-administration-built-migrant-cages-meme
-true/3413683001

39. https://www.federalregister.gov/documents/2021/02/05/2021
-02562/establishment-of-interagency-task-force-on-the
-reunification-of-families

40. https://www.nbcnews.com/politics/immigration/record-number
-unaccompanied-children-crossed-border-march-n1262901

41. https://thehill.com/opinion/immigration/550221-migrant
-children-suffering-the-unintended-consequences-of-biden
-policy

42. https://www.doctorswithoutborders.org/sites/default/files
/documents/Doctors%20Without%20Borders_No%20Way%20
Out%20Report.pdf

43. https://thespectator.info/2021/03/25/biden-says-migrant
-families-apprehended-at-border-should-all-be-going-back

44. https://www.heritage.org/immigration/commentary/bidens
-immigration-policies-have-turned-win-loss

45. https://www.hhs.gov/programs/social-services/unaccompanied -children/latest-uc-data-fy2021/index.html

46. https://www.borderreport.com/hot-topics/immigration/cbp-far -fewer-migrant-families-unaccompanied-children-came-across -the-border-in-october

47. https://abcnews.go.com/Health/covid-19-cases -unaccompanied-migrant-children-facilities-spark/story?id =76788478

48. https://www.bbc.com/news/world-us-canada-57149721

49. https://www.cbsnews.com/news/what-is-chain-migration -definition-visa-trump-administration-family-reunification

50. https://www.bbc.com/news/world-latin-america-40480405

51. https://www.courier-journal.com/story/news/investigations /2021/07/01/mexican-cartels-fuel-immigration-crisis-at-us -border/5290082001; https://www.citizensjournal.us/has-joe -biden-sold-out-america-to-the-mexican-drug-cartels

52. https://www.cbsnews.com/news/fentanyl-seizures-texas-mexico -border-immigration

53. https://www.cbp.gov/newsroom/stats/drug-seizure-statistics

54. https://www.newsweek.com/texas-sees-800-increase-fentanyl -coming-across-border-1594690

55. https://abcnews.go.com/Politics/fentanyl-seized-cbp-2021-2020 /story?id=77744071

56. https://spectator.org/fentanyl-overdoses-rising-2021

57. https://www.voanews.com/a/science-health_us-drug-overdose -deaths-hit-record-93000-last-year/6208259.html

58. Ibid.

59. https://www.kold.com/2021/06/11/biden-return-diverted -border-wall-money-spend-down-rest

60. https://www.whitehouse.gov/wp-content/uploads/2021/07 /Root-Causes-Strategy.pdf

61. https://www.mtsu.edu/first-amendment/post/1534/photos-of -migrant-detention-highlight-biden-s-border-secrecy

62. https://abcnews.go.com/Politics/photos-show-overcrowded -border-patrol-facility-texas/story?id=76604072

63. https://nypost.com/2021/03/12/biden-slammed-for-taking -credit-for-vaccine-not-thanking-trump

64. https://www.princetonpolicy.com/ppa-blog/2021/7/16/june-apprehensions-towards-worst-year-ever

65. https://www.nbcnews.com/politics/immigration/18-percent-migrant-families-leaving-border-patrol-custody-tested-positive-n1276244

66. https://www.msn.com/en-us/news/us/fact-check-are-covid-positive-migrants-allowed-to-cross-southern-border-into-us/ar-BB1ehZmr

67. https://travel.state.gov/content/travel/en/international-travel/before-you-go/covid-19_testing_required_US_Entry.html

68. https://www.msn.com/en-us/news/us/fact-check-are-covid-positive-migrants-allowed-to-cross-southern-border-into-us/ar-BB1ehZmr

69. https://www.foxnews.com/transcript/tucker-investigates-fulton-county-election-incident?cmpid=prn_newsstand

70. Ibid.

71. Ibid.

72. https://www.nytimes.com/2019/04/03/opinion/latino-voters.html

73. https://www.pewresearch.org/hispanic/2012/04/04/v-politics-values-and-religion

74. https://www.theblaze.com/news/dhs-secretary-border-crisis-children

75. https://www.politico.com/news/2021/07/13/mayorkas-cubans-haitians-499531

76. https://www.pewresearch.org/fact-tank/2020/10/02/most-cuban-american-voters-identify-as-republican-in-2020

77. https://www.latimes.com/projects/la-pol-ca-california-voting-history

78. https://www.ppic.org/publication/californias-population

79. https://fee.org/articles/california-has-the-highest-poverty-rate-in-america-why

80. https://www.sfgate.com/bayarea/article/rapporteur-United-Nations-San-Francisco-homeless-13351509.php

81. https://laist.com/news/hud-2018-homelessness-report

82. https://www.sandiegouniontribune.com/news/politics/sdut-welfare-capital-of-the-us-2012jul28-htmlstory.html

83. https://worldpopulationreview.com/state-rankings/least-educated-states

84. https://www.ocregister.com/2019/12/05/californias-disgraceful
-educational-test-scores-demand-action-gloria-romero
85. https://edsource.org/2020/less-than-a-third-of-california
-students-met-or-exceeded-standards-on-new-science-test/623514
86. https://news.yahoo.com/california-homicide-rise-becomes
-recall-120058030.html
87. https://news.yahoo.com/californias-prisons-jails-emptied
-thousands-120033846.html
88. https://www.disastercenter.com/crime/cacrime.htm
89. https://www.thecentersquare.com/california/list-of-companies
-leaving-california-grows-citing-high-tax-burden-cost-of-living
/article_b0add24a-753b-11eb-97bc-5bb1b2df1e43.html
90. https://www.thecentersquare.com/california/list-of-companies
-leaving-california-grows-citing-high-tax-burden-cost-of-living
/article_b0add24a-753b-11eb-97bc-5bb1b2df1e43.html; https://
marketrealist.com/p/california-companies-leaving

CHAPTER 5

1. https://www.politico.com/story/2008/11/exit-polls-how-obama
-won-015297
2. https://www.foxnews.com/politics/biden-channels-obama-in
-declaring-there-are-no-red-states-no-blue-states-just-the-united
-states
3. https://www.catholicleague.org/hating-whitey-is-in-vogue
4. https://libcom.org/files/Race%20Traitor%2009%20(1998%20
Summer).pdf
5. https://www.lohud.com/story/news/local/rockland/nyack/2019
/04/17/brinks-judith-clark-granted-parole-1981-robbery-murders
/3494841002
6. https://www.discoverthenetworks.org/individuals/chesa-boudin
7. https://www.nytimes.com/1993/11/18/garden/at-home-with
-bernadine-dohrn-same-passion-new-tactics.html?sq=Bernardine
+Dohrn&scp=1&st=cse
8. https://californiaglobe.com/section-2/movement-to-recall-san
-francisco-da-chesa-boudin-sees-support-donation-spikes-amid
-worsening-crime-wave
9. Stanely Kurtz, Radical in Chief: The Untold Story of Barack
Obama and American Socialism, 2010

10. https://www.investors.com/politics/columnists/obama-racism-is-in-american-dna

11. https://www.washingtonpost.com/outlook/2019/08/01/al-sharpton-is-not-lifelong-fighter-justice

12. https://www.discoverthenetworks.org/individuals/al-sharpton

13. https://www.foxnews.com/us/al-sharpton-gets-1m-in-pay-from-his-own-charity

14. https://www.rev.com/blog/transcripts/reverend-al-sharpton-eulogy-transcript-at-george-floyd-memorial-service

15. https://www.politico.com/story/2016/02/obama-civil-rights-meeting-219453

16. https://dfw.cbslocal.com/2016/07/08/chief-brown-dallas-shooting-suspect-wanted-to-kill-white-people

17. http://subwayreads.org/book/when-they-call-you-a-terrorist

18. Ibid.

19. https://nymag.com/intelligencer/2016/07/dallas-obama-straddles-the-divide.html

20. https://www.reuters.com/article/us-minneapolis-police-biden-bail-idUSKBN2360SZ

21. https://www.the-sun.com/news/1520376/black-lives-matter-bail-criminals-kamala-harris

22. Executive Order 13985, https://www.federalregister.gov/documents/2021/01/25/2021-01753/advancing-racial-equity-and-support-for-underserved-communities-through-the-federal-government

23. https://www.insider.com/four-minneapolis-police-officers-criminal-charges-george-floyd-death-2020-6

24. https://apnews.com/article/north-america-donald-trump-us-news-ap-top-news-keith-ellison-b95cf2336ba3481d88fc971ce347c940

25. David Horowitz, *"I Can't Breathe:" How A Racial Hoax Is Killing America*, Regnery 2021

26. https://www.breitbart.com/politics/2021/04/17/maxine-waters-derek-chauvin-must-be-guilty-guilty-guilty-or-we-take-to-the-streets

27. https://thehill.com/homenews/administration/549217-biden-praying-for-chauvin-conviction-evidence-overwhelming

28. https://www.baltimoresun.com/news/crime/bs-md-ci-baltimore-riots-what-we-know-20150428-story.html ; https://www

.theatlantic.com/politics/archive/2015/04/a-state-of-emergency
-in-baltimore/391607

29. Associated Press, Baltimore "Police Might Have Ignored Seat Belt
Policy with Freddie Gray," *Denver Post*, April 23, 2015, https://
www.denverpost.com/2015/04/23/baltimore-police-might
-have-ignored-seat-belt-policy-with-freddie-gray/ ; Associated
Press, "Thousands Expected at Monday's Funeral for Freddie
Gray," Breitbart, April 27, 2015, https://www.breitbart.com
/news/thousands-expected-at-mondays-funeral-for-freddie-gray;
German Lopez, "The Baltimore Protests over Freddie Gray's
Death, Explained," Vox, August 18, 2016, https://www.vox.com
/2016/7/27/18089352/freddie-gray-baltimore-riots-police-violence

30. https://www.theguardian.com/commentisfree/2016/jul/27
/freddie-gray-decision-black-lives-matter

31. Larry Elder (@larryelder), "Freddie Gray Died (2015)," Twitter,
June 6, 2020, 8:49 PM, https://twitter.com/larryelder
/status/1269431344569802752?lang=en

32. https://www.britannica.com/topic/critical-race-theory

33. https://abcnews.go.com/Politics/joe-biden-white-america-admit
-systemic-racism/story?id=60524966

34. https://www.nytimes.com/1970/05/25/archives/a-radical
-declaration-warns-of-an-attack-by-weathermen.html

35. The history of this movement and its deceptions can be found
in David Horowitz, *"I Can't Breathe:" How a Racial Hoax is Killing
America*, Regnery 2021

36. https://www.washingtontimes.com/news/2020/jun/3/liberal
-politicians-who-order-police-to-stand-down

37. https://nypost.com/2020/06/04/gov-andrew-cuomos-full-of-it
-on-looters-and-the-no-bail-law

38. https://www.the-sun.com/news/1520376/black-lives-matter-bail
-criminals-kamala-harris

39. https://www.discoverthenetworks.org/individuals/joe-biden

40. https://www.dailysignal.com/2019/11/12/san-franciscos-new-da
-public-urination-will-not-be-prosecuted; https://stanfordreview
.org/chesa-boudin-san-franciscos-lawless-revolutionary

41. https://www.jacobinmag.com/2019/05/chesa-boudin-san
-francisco-district-attorney

42. https://www.nbcchicago.com/news/local/black-lives-matter -holds-rally-supporting-individuals-arrested-in-chicago-looting -monday/2320365
43. https://www.mystateline.com/news/national/chicago-black-lives -matter-defends-looting-as-reparations-for-oppression
44. https://www.abc10.com/article/news/local/california/70000 -violent-career-felons-to-get-earlier-releases/103-eb4e7578-f7f1 -44cc-aef8-b924ed97f7e8
45. https://nypost.com/2020/06/28/nypd-animosity-towards-police -is-driving-spike-in-shootings
46. https://abcnews.go.com/US/us-cities-increase-violent-crime -police-group/story?id=71411919
47. https://nypost.com/2020/06/26/minneapolis-city-council -approves-measure-to-abolish-police-force
48. https://www.nytimes.com/2020/07/21/us/minneapolis-police -george-floyd-protests.html
49. https://www.upi.com/Top_News/US/2021/06/17/Portland -Police-disband-Rapid-Response-Team/2481623968649
50. https://www.wsj.com/articles/nypd-disbands-anticrime-unit -as-city-leaders-debate-1-billion-in-cuts-to-police -11592263500
51. https://www.bloomberg.com/graphics/2021-city-budget-police -funding
52. https://www.breitbart.com/clips/2020/07/01/de-blasio-doubles -down-on-threat-to-paint-black-lives-matter-in-front-of-trump -tower-vows-to-use-defunded-police-money-to-pay-for-it
53. https://www.ibtimes.com/Squad-member-cori-bush-spent-70k -private-security-even-she-called-defund-police-3259364
54. https://www.npr.org/2021/01/06/953254623/massive-1-year -rise-in-homicide-rates-collided-with-the-pandemic-in-2020; https://twitter.com/Crimealytics/status/1343950694672379905 /photo/1
55. https://www.city-journal.org/ferguson-effect-inner-cities
56. https://ucr.fbi.gov/crime-in-the-u.s/2019/crime-in-the-u.s.-2019 /topic-pages/tables/table-43
57. Ibid.
58. https://nypost.com/2021/08/11/sen-cory-booker-gives-satirical -defund-the-police-speech-on-senate-floor

59. https://nypost.com/2021/06/23/biden-to-blame-crimewave-on
    -guns-rather-than-post-protest-tolerance-for-lawlessness

60. https://reason.com/2020/08/06/81-percent-of-black-americans
    -want-the-same-level-or-more-of-police-presence-gallup; https://
    news.gallup.com/poll/316571/black-americans-police-retain
    -local-presence.aspx?utm_source=tagrss&utm_medium=rss&utm
    _campaign=syndication

61. https://www.foxnews.com/media/dc-police-chief-justice-system
    -coddle-violent-criminals

CHAPTER 6

1. https://www.foxnews.com/politics/top-democrats-fume-after
   -trump-expands-travel-restrictions-six-new-countries; https://
   www.frontpagemag.com/fpm/2020/03/coronavirus-and-dam
   -thats-been-broken-dennis-prager

2. https://www.washingtonexaminer.com/news/los-angeles-times
   -and-bloomberg-news-federal-stockpile-of-n95-masks-was
   -depleted-under-obama-and-never-restocked

3. https://www.nytimes.com/2020/03/18/us/politics/china-virus.html

4. https://www.newsweek.com/biden-trump-has-given-fighting
   -coronavirus-1541795

5. https://www.washingtonpost.com/politics/biden-trump
   -coronavirus-vaccine/2020/09/16/2ffbea6a-f831-11ea-a275
   -1a2c2d36e1f1_story.html. See also https://www.msn.com/en-us
   /entertainment/news/kamala-harris-says-she-wouldnt-trust-a
   -vaccine-trump-recommended/ar-BB19O9k4

6. https://nypost.com/2020/10/07/kamala-harris-on-covid-vaccine
   -wont-take-it-trump-tells-me-to

7. https://thehill.com/opinion/white-house/544175-getting-the
   -facts-right-on-operation-warp-speed

8. https://slate.com/news-and-politics/2008/08/the-wacky
   -plagiarisms-of-joe-biden.html

9. https://www.whitehouse.gov/briefing-room/speeches-remarks
   /2021/03/11/remarks-by-president-biden-on-the-anniversary-of
   -the-covid-19-shutdown

10. https://www.reuters.com/article/uk-factcheck-fauci-outdated
    -video-masks/fact-checkoutdated-video-of-fauci-saying-theres
    -no-reason-to-be-walking-around-with-a-mask-idUSKBN26T2TR

11. https://www.nbcnews.com/politics/2020-election/if-president
    -biden-would-seek-require-americans-wear-mask-public-n1232209

12. See https://www.nejm.org/doi/full/10.1056/nejmp2006372.
    However, the authors of the NEJM study later clarified their
    views, seemingly under intense political pressure, to say that
    they did believe mask-wearing could be helpful in "sustained
    interactions within closed environments." https://www.nejm.org
    /doi/full/10.1056/NEJMc2020836

13. https://finance.yahoo.com/quote/%5EDJI/history?period1
    =1471996800&period2=1629763200&interval=1d&filter=history
    &frequency=1d&includeAdjustedClose=true

14. https://www.cnn.com/2020/03/29/politics/trump-coronavirus
    -press-conference/index.html

15. https://www.cnn.com/2020/03/31/us/violating-coronavirus
    -orders-trnd/index.html

16. https://trumpwhitehouse.archives.gov/articles/15-days-slow
    -spread. See also https://www.livescience.com/coronavirus
    -flatten-the-curve.html; https://dailycaller.com/2021/04/21
    /covid-19-coronavirus-lockdowns-hospitalizations-flatten
    -the-curve

17. https://www.cnbc.com/2020/06/16/pelosi-says-advertisers
    -should-push-platforms-to-combat-disinformation.html

18. https://www.ndtv.com/world-news/social-media
    -misinformation-on-covid-killing-people-joe-biden-2488477

19. https://www.poynter.org/reporting-editing/2020/where-does
    -the-government-get-2-trillion-for-a-coronavirus-bailout

20. https://www.investopedia.com/coronavirus-aid-relief-and
    -economic-security-cares-act-4800707; https://www.newyorklife
    .com/newsroom/coronavirus-tony-malloy-federal-stimulus

21. https://www.investopedia.com/coronavirus-aid-relief-and
    -economic-security-cares-act-4800707

22. https://www.npr.org/2021/02/26/971438274/democrats-say
    -relief-programs-could-become-this-generations-new-deal

23. https://edition.cnn.com/2021/05/26/politics/6-trillion-stimulus
    -where-it-went/index.html; https://www.dol.gov/agencies/whd
    /pandemic/ffcra-employee-paid-leave; https://www.congress.gov
    /bill/116th-congress/house-bill/266/text

24. https://twitter.com/AnandDoobay/status/1248607946638077952
25. https://gis.cdc.gov/grasp/CovidNet/Covid19_3.html
26. https://www.npr.org/2021/02/06/964822479/supreme-court
    -rules-against-california-ban-on-in-person-worship-amid-the
    -pandemi. https://www.kusi.com/california-highway-patrol
    -bans-rallies-and-protests-due-to-coronavirus-lockdown. See also
    https://www.theblaze.com/news/san-bernardino-bans-church
    -for-easter-fine-jail; https://uk.finance.yahoo.com/video
    /federal-judge-says-york-officials-011220521.html?
27. https://fee.org/articles/california-has-the-strictest-lockdown-in
    -the-us-and-the-most-active-Covid-cases-by-far
28. https://datavisualizations.heritage.org/public-health/covid-19
    -death-rates-by-state
29. https://datavisualizations.heritage.org/public-health/covid-19
    -death-rates-by-state
30. https://news.yahoo.com/trump-says-china-either
    -could-212804593.html
31. https://www.cnbc.com/2020/03/18/coronavirus-criticism
    -trump-defends-saying-chinese-virus.html
32. https://www.thelancet.com/journals/lancet/article/PIIS0140
    -6736(20)30418-9/fulltext
33. https://www.science.org/doi/10.1126/science.abj0016
34. https://www.washingtonexaminer.com/opinion/politifact
    -retracts-wuhan-lab-theory-fact-check
35. https://www.msn.com/en-us/health/medical/politifact-retracts
    -wuhan-lab-theory-fact-check/ar-AAKgsZg
36. https://www.wsj.com/articles/intelligence-on-sick-staff-at-wuhan
    -lab-fuels-debate-on-covid-19-origin-11621796228?mod
    =djemalertNEWS
37. https://www.nature.com/articles/d41586-017-08837-7
38. https://www.washingtonexaminer.com/news/fauci-denies-nih
    -supported-gain-of-function-research-wuhan-lab
39. https://27m3p2uv7igmj6kvd4ql3cct5h3sdwrsajovkkndeufumzy
    fhlfev4qd.onion/2021/09/06/new-details-emerge-about
    -coronavirus-research-at-chinese-lab
40. https://reporter.nih.gov/project-details/8674931
41. https://reporter.nih.gov/project-details/8674931

42. https://www.washingtonpost.com/politics/2021/05/18/fact
-checking-senator-paul-dr-fauci-flap-over-wuhan-lab-funding.
See also the published report itself, https://journals.plos.org
/plospathogens/article?id=10.1371/journal.ppat.1006698

43. On May 19, 2021, the NIH released a statement to the
Washington Post that reiterated its position that it never funded
gain of function research in China. "NIH has never approved any
grant to support 'gain-of-function' research on coronaviruses
that would have increased their transmissibility or lethality for
humans. The research proposed in the EcoHealth Alliance, Inc.
grant application sought to understand how bat coronaviruses
evolve naturally in the environment to become transmissible to
the human population." https://www.scribd.com/document
/508545947/NIH-Statement-May-19-2021

44. https: https://news.yahoo.com/internal-documents-further
-contradict-fauci-142902303.html//news.yahoo.com/internal
-documents-further-contradict-fauci-142902303.html

45. https://news.yahoo.com/internal-documents-further-contradict
-fauci-142902303.html

46. https://nypost.com/2021/06/02/fauci-was-warned-that-covid
-may-have-been-engineered-emails

47. https://reason.com/2021/07/23/is-anthony-fauci-lying-about
-nih-funding-of-wuhan-lab-research-or-is-rand-paul

48. https://www.dailywire.com/news/biden-demonizes-unvaccinated
-people-they-are-sowing-enormous-confusion-not-nearly-as
-smart-as-i-thought

49. https://nypost.com/2021/08/30/arne-duncan-compares-anti
-maskers-to-kabul-suicide-bomber; https://nypost.com/2021/08/27
/pentagon-only-one-suicide-bomb-exploded-in-kabul-airport
-attack

50. https://townhall.com/tipsheet/zachbauder/2021/07/26/gavin
-newsome-unvaccinated-are-like-drunk-drivers-n2593133

51. https://www.msn.com/en-us/news/politics/nancy-pelosi
-calls-unvaccinated-members-of-congress-a-danger
/ar-AAKdoUq

52. https://www.newsweek.com/joe-biden-speech-july-4
-instructions-cdc-warning-backlash-twitter-1575634

53. https://usafacts.org/visualizations/coronavirus-covid-19-spread-map

54. https://www.bbc.com/news/world-us-canada-55193939

55. https://abcnews.go.com/Politics/biden-speak-vaccine-politics-center-stage-process/story?id=73047767

56. https://www.foxnews.com/media/cnn-don-lemon-rules-force-vaccinations-freedom-liberty

57. https://www.washingtonpost.com/business/2021/07/27/biden-vaccine-mandate-federal-employees

58. https://www.msn.com/en-us/health/medical/study-cited-by-cdc-to-justify-new-mask-guidance-rejected-by-peer-review-based-on-vaccine-not-used-in-us/ar-AAMFY8P

59. https://reason.com/2021/08/04/the-evidence-cited-by-the-cdc-does-not-show-that-vaccinated-and-unvaccinated-covid-19-carriers-are-equally-likely-to-transmit-the-virus

60. https://www.cdc.gov/vaccines/covid-19/health-departments/breakthrough-cases.html. See also https://americanactionnews.com/featured/2021/08/06/biden-cdc-used-fake-study-to-call-for-mask-mandate-rs-mb; https://www.healthline.com/health-news/covid-19-by-the-numbers-vaccinated-continue-to-be-protected

61. https://www.cnet.com/health/cdc-and-who-recommend-fully-vaccinated-should-wear-masks-indoors-heres-the-latest. See also https://www.nbcnews.com/news/us-news/cdc-recommends-masks-all-k-12-students-even-those-who-n1275173

62. https://townhall.com/tipsheet/spencerbrown/2021/08/02/mixed-messages-psaki-insists-biden-isnt-shutting-down-america-again-n2593478

63. https://www.washingtonpost.com/health/2021/03/28/vaccine-passports-for-work

64. https://thehill.com/opinion/finance/565860-coming-soon-americas-own-social-credit-system

65. https://abc7ny.com/nyc-vaccine-passport-requirement-mandate-Covid/10926728

66. http://www.cnn.com/TRANSCRIPTS/2108/03/cg.01.html

67. https://abc7ny.com/nyc-vaccine-passport-requirement-mandate-Covid/10926728

68. https://freerepublic.com/focus/f-bloggers/3980862/posts

69. https://nypost.com/2010/06/18/7-a-gallon-gas

70. Václav Havel, *The Power of the Powerless* (New York: Vintage, 1979), p. 37.

71. https://www.npr.org/2021/08/02/1023637178/many-states-are -trying-to-prevent-vaccine-mandate-laws; https://www.chn.org /voices/covid-watch-august-6-2021

72. https://abcnews.go.com/Health/businesses-mandating-covid-19 -vaccines-legal/story?id=79223479

73. https://www.nashp.org/state-lawmakers-submit-bills-to-ban -employer-vaccine-mandates

74. https://www.whitehouse.gov/briefing-room/speeches-remarks/2021 /08/03/remarks-by-president-biden-on-fighting-the-covid-19 -pandemic

75. https://www.libertynation.com/desantis-v-biden-in-a-battle-for -hearts-and-minds/#:~:text=On%20one%20side%20is%20President %20Joe%20Biden%2C%20who,and%20the%20media%20 united%20against%20his%20political%20future

76. https://www.foxnews.com/media/desantis-biden-covid-variant -open-border

77. https://www.rev.com/blog/transcripts/fl-gov-ron-desantis -response-to-joe-biden-transcript-why-dont-you-do-your-job

CHAPTER 7

1. *Guardian*, April 12, 2020 cited in Marc Morano. *Green Fraud: Why the Green New Deal Is Even Worse than You Think* Kindle Edition, p. 194

2. Morano, op. cit., p. 196

3. Morano, op. cit., p. 198

4. Morano, op. cit., p. 203

5. https://www.insidesources.com/bigname-2020-dems-support -the-green-new-deal-but-big-name-enviro-groups-don't; https:// www.markey.senate.gov/news/press-releases/senator-markey -and-rep-ocasio-cortez-introduce-green-new-deal-resolution; https://www.breitbart.com/politics/2019/02/19/whos-behind -the-green-new-deal-big-money-backs-ocasio-cortez-socialist -dream-project; https://twitter.com/sunrisemvmt/status /1075411614860492805?ref_src=

6. https://www.npr.org/2019/02/07/691997301/rep-alexandria-ocasio-cortez-releases-green-new-deal-outline

7. https://www.heartland.org/news-opinion/news/how-to-defeat-the-democrats-dangerous-green-new-deal

8. Ibid.

9. https://s3.documentcloud.org/documents/5729035/Green-New-Deal-FAQ.pdf

10. https://theconversation.com/green-new-deal-universal-basic-income-could-make-green-transition-feasible-112898

11. https://www.seattletimes.com/opinion/nuclear-energy-can-make-a-carbon-free-future-a-reality

12. https://www.whitehouse.gov/briefing-room/presidential-actions/2021/01/20/executive-order-protecting-public-health-and-environment-and-restoring-science-to-tackle-climate-crisis

13. https://www.foxnews.com/politics/bidens-keystone-xl-gina-mccarthy-jobs-sacrifice

14. https://www.npr.org/2021/05/28/1000843544/biden-proposes-a-huge-hike-in-government-spending-in-a-6-trillion-budget

15. https://www.investopedia.com/american-rescue-plan-definition-5095694

16. https://www.wsj.com/articles/biden-set-to-unveil-2-trillion-infrastructure-plan-11617181208

17. https://www.nytimes.com/2021/08/11/us/politics/senate-budget-plan.html

18. https://www.heritage.org/budget-and-spending/commentary/5-things-you-need-know-about-bidens-18-trillion-american-families

19. https://exhibitcitynews.com/how-big-is-one-trillion-dollars

20. https://www.breitbart.com/economy/2021/08/09/june-jolts

21. https://www.resourcestaff.com/report-the-bls-employment-situation-june-2021

22. https://www.bls.gov/iag/tgs/iag722.htm

23. https://www.noradarealestate.com/blog/housing-market-predictions; https://talkbusiness.net/2021/06/meat-prices-rise-to-record-levels

24. https://www.cnbc.com/2021/04/28/biden-promises-no-new-taxes-on-anyone-making-less-than-400000.html

25. Google dictionary.

26. https://www.cnn.com/2021/03/04/politics/stimulus-senate -democrats-proposal/index.html

27. https://nypost.com/2021/08/09/one-awful-bill-one-terrible-bill -hope-that-dems-double-dealing-dooms-them-both

28. https://nypost.com/2021/08/09/one-awful-bill-one-terrible-bill -hope-that-dems-double-dealing-dooms-them-both

29. https://www.heritage.org/welfare/commentary/bait-and-switch -biden-child-allowance-tax-relief-overturns-welfare-reform

30. Ibid.

31. Ibid.

32. https://budgetmodel.wharton.upenn.edu/issues/2021/4/23 /revenue-effects-of-president-bidens-capital-gains-tax-increase

33. https://www.forbes.com/sites/markhendrickson/2012/07/19 /obama-strays-from-the-script-reveals-an-ideology-hed-prefer-to -hide/?sh=387e19d06aa1

34. Federalist #10

CHAPTER 8

1. https://cicilline.house.gov/press-release/cicilline-merkley -announce-introduction-equality-act

2. https://www.heritage.org/gender/commentary/woke-gender

3. "The Inequality of the Equality Act: Concerns from the Left." This is a panel of lifelong left-wing activists and formerly transgendered individuals. https://www.youtube.com/watch?v=HMj9MOuRswc

4. https://thefederalist.com/2015/08/19/transgender-regret-is -real-even-if-the-media-tell-you-otherwise; https://quillette .com/2020/01/02/the-ranks-of-gender-detransitioners-are -growing-we-need-to-understand-why

5. https//www.wsj.com/articles/SB1041302509432817073

6. https//www.wsj.com/articles/SB1041302509432817073

7. https://www.legislationline.org/download/id/1472/file /3b50795b2d0374cbef5c29766256.pdf

8. https://fortune.com/2021/01/20/kamala-harris-vp-senate -tiebreaker-biden

9. https://search.yahoo.com/yhs/search?hspart=tro&hsimp=yhs -freshy&grd=1&type=Y219_F163_204671_033021&p=Georgia +senators&rdr=1&guccounter=1

10. https://www.dailysignal.com/2020/11/20/7-ways-the-2005-carter
-baker-report-could-have-averted-problems-with-2020-election

11. https://ultraltd.net/w2dl9/ca7301-georgia-election-law
-changes-2020

12. https://www.judicialwatch.org/tom-fittons-weekly-update
/new-election-lawsuits; https://nationalfile.com/lawsuit-georgia
-sec-of-state-signed-illegal-deal-with-democrats-changing-how
-ballots-are-processed; https://www.theblaze.com/op-ed/levin
-on-january-6-we-learn-whether-our-constitution-will-hold

13. https://thefederalist.com/2020/05/26/spygate-law-firm-that
-attempted-to-overturn-2016-election-behind-2020-voting
-lawsuits

14. https://www.theblaze.com/op-ed/levin-on-january-6-we-learn
-whether-our-constitution-will-hold; https://www.happyscribe
.com/public/mark-levin-podcast/20-312700f3-893f-4822-a04b
-c8c6bdf941af

15. https://www.ajc.com/politics/turnout-dip-among-georgia-republicans
-flipped-us-senate/IKWGEGFEEVEZ5DXTP7ZXXOROIA

16. https://www.dailywire.com/news/trump-camps-georgia-lawsuit
-alleges-massive-fraud-here-are-the-details

17. https://ballotpedia.org/Election_integrity#Georgia_Election
_Integrity_Act_of_2021

18. https://www.whitehouse.gov/briefing-room/speeches-remarks
/2021/03/25/remarks-by-president-biden-in-press-conference

19. https://www.post-gazette.com/news/nation/2021/03/27/Biden
-attacks-new-Georgia-voting-law/stories/202103280126; https://
www.washingtonexaminer.com/politics/how-georgias-new
-voting-law-compares-to-other-states

20. https://www.marketwatch.com/story/stacey-abrams-on-voting
-rights-georgia-election-law-and-her-next-move-01617981511

21. https://www.nationalreview.com/2021/03/the-voter-suppression
-lie

22. https://www.heritage.org/election-integrity/impact/georgia
-adopts-voter-reforms-based-heritage-recommendations

23. https://www.heritage.org/election-integrity/impact/georgia
-adopts-voter-reforms-based-heritage-recommendations

24. https://www.heritage.org/election-integrity/impact/georgia
-adopts-voter-reforms-based-heritage-recommendations

25. https://www.heritage.org/press/heritage-foundation-releases
-fact-check-georgia-election-reform-law; https://www.legis.ga.gov
/api/legislation/document/20212022/201121; https://www
.heritage.org/election-integrity/commentary/the-truth-about
-georgias-voting-law

26. https://www.heritage.org/press/heritage-foundation-releases-fact
-check-georgia-election-reform-law; https://www.legis.ga.gov/api
/legislation/document/20212022/201121; https://www.heritage
.org/election-integrity/commentary/the-truth-about-georgias
-voting-law

27. https://www.whitehouse.gov/briefing-room/speeches-remarks
/2021/03/26/remarks-by-president-biden-before-marine-one
-departure

28. https://www.washingtonexaminer.com/politics/how-georgias
-new-voting-law-compares-to-other-states

29. https://www.discoverthenetworks.org/organizations/h-r-1-the
-for-the-people-act-of-2021; https://dailycaller.com/2021/03/04
/house-passed-hr-1-for-people-act; https://www.legislationline.org
/download/id/1472/file/3b50795b2d0374cbef5c29766256.pdf;
https://theintercept.com/2021/08/11/joe-manchin-voting
-rights-bill

30. https://www.discoverthenetworks.org/organizations/h-r-1-the
-for-the-people-act-of-2021; https://dailycaller.com/2021/03/04
/house-passed-hr-1-for-people-act; https://www.legislationline.org
/download/id/1472/file/3b50795b2d0374cbef5c29766256.pdf;
https://theintercept.com/2021/08/11/joe-manchin-voting
-rights-bill

31. https://www.foxnews.com/politics/democratic-rep-hank
-johnson-arrested-by-capitol-police-during-protest

32. https://www.breitbart.com/clips/2021/08/12/eric-holder
-citizens-need-to-be-in-streets-getting-arrested-over-voting
-rights

33. Ibid.

CHAPTER 9

1. Carol Leonnig; Philip Rucker, *I Alone Can Fix It*, Penguin Press,
2021. The authors are *Washington Post* reporters.

2. https://abcnews.go.com/Politics/pelosi-announces-select
   -committee-investigate-jan-assault-capitol/story?id=78465513
3. https://www.msnbc.com/opinion/why-ron-desantis-more
   -dangerous-trump-n1276142; https://news.yahoo.com/white
   -house-seizes-opportunity-whack-212325032.html?fr=yhssrp
   _catchall
4. Lee Smith, *The Plot Against the President: The True Story of How
   Congressman Devin Nunes Uncovered the Biggest Political Scandal in
   U.S. History* (2019); Gregg Jarrett, *The Russia Hoax: The Illicit Scheme
   to Clear Hillary Clinton and Frame Donald Trump* (2019); Dan
   Bongino, *Spygate: The Attempted Sabotage of Donald J. Trump* (2019).
5. https://www.frontpagemag.com/fpm/2021/08/disloyal
   -frontpagemagcom
6. Ibid.
7. https://thehill.com/homenews/administration/560348-trump
   -aides-drafted-order-to-invoke-insurrection-act-during-floyd
8. https://www.usatoday.com/story/news/politics/2021/06/28
   /milley-trump-had-confrontation-over-protest-response-book
   -reveals/5369959001
9. Matthew Lohmeier, *Irresistible Revolution: Marxism's Goal of
   Conquest & the Unmaking of the American Military*, May 2021
10. Daniel Greenfield, *Disloyal: How the Military Brass Is Betraying
    Our Country*, David Horowitz Freedom Center, Sherman Oaks
    California, 2021
11. https://thefederalist.com/2020/08/06/gallup-81-percent-of
    -black-americans-want-police-protection-some-want-more
12. https://www.defense.gov/Explore/News/Article/Article/2573268
    /biden-announces-full-us-troop-withdrawal-from-afghanistan
    -by-sept-11
13. https://apnews.com/article/joe-biden-afghanistan-government
    -and-politics-86f939c746c7bc56bb9f11f095a95366
14. https://www.wsj.com/articles/bidens-message-on-afghanistan
    -withdrawal-draws-critics-11629889203; https://www
    .washingtonpost.com/national-security/2021/08/10
    /afghanistan-intelligence-assessment
15. https://thenewamerican.com/reuters-biden-told-ghani-to-lie
    -about-strength-of-afghan-troops

16. https://www.whitehouse.gov/briefing-room/speeches-remarks
/2021/07/08/remarks-by-president-biden-on-the-drawdown-of
-u-s-forces-in-afghanistan

17. https://www.theepochtimes.com/mkt_breakingnews/taliban
-seizes-presidential-palace-to-soon-declare-islamic-emirate-of
-afghanistan_3949578.html

18. https://www.axios.com/taliban-bagram-prisoners-release
-87ec6885-6930-46d6-9e96-473a252dcf7d.html

19. https://www.pbs.org/newshour/politics/u-s-left-afghan-airfield
-at-night-didnt-tell-new-commander

20. https://nypost.com/2021/08/20/us-left-billions-in-weapons-in
-afghanistan-with-black-hawks-in-talibans-hands

21. https://justthenews.com/government/white-house/us-leaving
-behind-75000-vehicles-600000-weapons-and-208-planes
-afghanistan

22. https://www.politico.com/news/2021/08/26/us-officials
-provided-taliban-with-names-of-americans-afghan-allies-to
-evacuate-506957

23. https://www.nbcnews.com/news/world/high-threat-terror
-attack-disrupts-kabul-airport-evacuations-biden-deadline
-n1277670

24. https://en.wikipedia.org/wiki/2021_Kabul_airport_attack

25. https://americanpeopledaily.com/pelosi-stands-strong-in
-her-unbelievable-praise-for-the-presidents-actions-in
-afghanistan

26. https://media.defense.gov/2021/Apr/09/2002617921/-1/-1/1
/MEMORANDUM-IMMEDIATE-ACTIONS-TO-COUNTER
-EXTREMISM-IN-THE-DEPARTMENT-AND-THE
-ESTABLISHMENT-OF-THE-COUNTERING-EXTREMISM
-WORKING-GROUP.PDF

27. https://www.fox5dc.com/news/25000-national-guard-troops
-deployed-to-capitol-as-biden-inauguration-looms

28. https://www.defense.gov/Explore/News/Article/Article/2492530
/austin-orders-military-stand-down-to-address-challenge-of
-extremism-in-the-ranks

29. https://www.msn.com/en-us/news/opinion/gen-mark-milley-i
-want-to-understand-white-rage-and-im-white/ar-AALmRg1

30. https://www.jihadwatch.org/2021/06/pelosi-root-causes-of
-capitol-insurrection-were-white-supremacy-anti-semitism
-islamophobia-2

CHAPTER 10

1. Eric Williams, Ed. D., Superintendents' Equity Statement,"
cited in https://www.lcps.org/Page/219268 Nate Hochman,
"The Battle of Loudon County," *The American Mind,* June 11,
2021.
2. https://shenviapologetics.com/quotes-from-applebaums-being
-white-being-good
3. Cited in https://cplaction.com/wp-content/uploads/CRT
-Briefing-Book-Rufo.pdf
4. https://news.yahoo.com/judge-rules-loudoun-county-teen
-131413442.html
5. https://nypost.com/2021/10/22/loudoun-county-school-boss
-scott-ziegler-knew-of-alleged-sex-assault-report
6. https://news.yahoo.com/loudoun-county-dad-says-daughter
-174943270.html
7. https://www.washingtonexaminer.com/news/justice/doj-talked
-with-white-house-before-issuing-domestic-terrorism-school
-protest-memo
8. https://uncoverdc.com/2021/10/05/nsba-letter-some-parents
-actions-could-be-form-of-domestic-terrorism
9. https://www.justice.gov/ag/page/file/1438986/download
10. https://redstate.com/nick-arama/2021/10/27/josh-hawley
-lights-up-merrick-garland-over-new-troubling-memo-against
-parents-n464486
11. https://www.forbes.com/sites/nicholasreimann/2021/10/27
/resign-in-disgrace-gop-senators-blast-garland-over-investigating
-threats-against-school-boards/?sh=7abd31fc6a26
12. https://www.washingtonpost.com/local/virginia-politics
/virginia-governor-poll-wason-center/2021/08/25/ccf18426-05f3
-11ec-a654-900a78538242_story.html
13. https://news.yahoo.com/mcauliffe-says-parents-shouldn-t
-173500644.html
14. https://www.youtube.com/watch?v=OzJYeVm65DE

15. https://www.msn.com/en-us/news/us/black-mother-compares-critical-race-theory-in-schools-to-kkk-tactics/ar-BB1gHtMa
16. https://ballotpedia.org/State_legislative_elections,_2021
17. https://www.newsmax.com/newsfront/new-jersey-legislature-edward-durr-senate/2021/11/04/id/1043330
18. https://www.nbcnews.com/politics/politics-news/nj-governor-race-2021-phil-murphy-n1282924
19. https://www.governing.com/now/its-not-that-democrats-lost-its-that-they-lost-everywhere
20. https://www.poconorecord.com/story/news/politics/elections/local/2021/11/03/democrats-defeated-gop-candidates-del-val-school-board/6266692001
21. https://www.nbcnews.com/news/education/school-board-candidates-opposed-critical-race-theory-mask-mandates-win-rcna4420
22. https://www.columbian.com/news/2021/nov/03/defund-the-police-candidates-stumble-in-liberal-seattle
23. https://www.foxnews.com/us/minneapolis-police-ballot-measure
24. https://www.reuters.com/world/us/biden-returns-sobering-virginia-upset-democrat-battle-congress-2021-11-03
25. https://www.rev.com/blog/transcripts/winsome-sears-wins-virginia-lt-gov-speech-transcript
26. https://www.foxnews.com/media/liberal-dyson-msnbc-joy-reid-winsome-sears-black-mouth-white-supremacist
27. https://townhall.com/tipsheet/katiepavlich/2021/07/13/oops-clyburn-admits-the-voting-thing-is-about-keeping-democrats-in-power-n2592435
28. https://www.politico.com/news/2021/07/26/democrats-gop-voting-laws-crisis-500726

CHAPTER 11
1. https://thehill.com/homenews/administration/560348-trump-aides-drafted-order-to-invoke-insurrection-act-during-floyd
2. Carol Leonnig, Rucker, Philip. *I Alone Can Fix It* Kindle Edition., p. 435
3. Ibid.
4. Leonnig and Rucker, op., cit. pp. 436–437

5. Ibid.
6. Ibid.
7. https://www.foxnews.com/opinion/tucker-carlson-chairman-joint
    -chiefs-of-staff-should-be-fired; https://www.cnbc.com/2021/07
    /15/mark-milley-feared-coup-after-trump-lost-to-biden-book
    .html; https://thehill.com/blogs/blog-briefing-room
    /news/563200-trump-milley-last-person-ld-start-a-coup-with
8. Leonnig and Rucker op. cit., pp. 498–499.
9. Ibid.
10. Ibid.
11. Leonnig and Rucker, op. cit. Kindle edition pp. 498–499
12. Fox News, op. cit.

Index

Abortion, 159
Abraham Accords, 48
Abrams, Stacey, 165
Affordable Care Act, 144
Afghanistan. *See* Fall of Afghanistan
al-Baghdadi, Abu Bakr, 40
Amazing Magnets, 90
America
    borders. *See* Open borders
    citizenship process, 61
    Cubans in U.S., 87
    deeply divided on issues of life, liberty, and pursuit of happiness, 156
    falsification of America's history, 49–54
    founding fathers, 1–2, 153
    Hispanic Americans, 85, 86
    nation founded by conservative realists, 153
    racial equality/racial flaws, 53
    systemic racism, 54–56
    "white supremacy," 55
American Enterprise Institute, 179
American Families Plan, 145
American Rescue Plan, 145, 146
American Rescue Plan Act, 59
Animal Farm (Orwell), 151
Antifa, 39, 98
Anti-white racism, 96
Apple, 90
Applebaum, Barbara, 194
Apprehensions of illegal aliens, 66–67, 72
Asher, Jeff, 108
Asian Americans, 54–55
Assimilation, 63
Atkins, Ariel, 105
Atkins, David, 37
Atkisson, Sharyl, 70
Atlanta Journal-Constitution, 163
Austin, Lloyd, 178, 179, 188, 189
Ayers, Bill, 93–94

Babbitt, Ashli, 23, 174
Bagram Air Base, 183–184
Baker, James, 5
Ballot dumps, 8–9
Barr, William, 13

Being White, Being Good (Applebaum), 194
Biden, Joe
  accusing Trump of killing COVID-19
    patients, 10
  administering COVID-19 relief on
    racist basis, 59
  assimilation, illegal aliens, 63
  boasting that he would beat Trump
    and rebuild nation, 60
  border wall, 66, 67
  Build Back Better initiative, 200
  cancellation of Keystone Pipeline, 142
  cancelling 1776 Commission project,
    49, 52, 54
  cancelling Trump's priority of
    deporting illegal aliens, 68
  claiming federal government had
    monopoly on the truth, 137
  Congressional Gold Medal awards to
    Capitol police officers, 171
  demonizing the unvaxxed, 130
  dismissing Antifa as merely "an idea," 39
  downplaying seriousness of COVID-19
    pandemic, 115
  equity, 56
  executive actions to reverse Trump
    policies, 46, 47, 68
  farm relief program, 59
  George Floyd case, 99–100
  inauguration speech, 46
  indictment of America as racist nation,
    54
  integration, undocumented immigrants, 63
  "Jim Crow 2," 167
  "Jim Crow on steroids," 165
  little credibility, 192
  new grant priority for American
    History and Civic Education
    programs, 52
  Nord Stream gas pipeline, 143
  "On Advancing Racial Equity," 56
  Palestinian terrorists, 48–49
  plagiarizing speeches and articles of
    other politicians, 117
  portraying himself as nation's savior
    while saying his opponents are
    misinformed, 136
  racist equity agenda, 59
  redistribution of wealth, 56, 57
  rejoining WHO, 47
  repealing Trump's key policies, 66
  response to coronavirus, 130, 132

  revealing how extreme his agenda
    actually was, 38
  reversal of 62 Trump orders, 68
  spiking crime rates, 112
  systemic racism, 103
  Task Force on the Reunification of
    Families, 75
  "Trump's vaccine," 116
  See also Open borders; 2020 presidential
    election
Biden administration. *See* Biden, Joe
"Big Lie," 32
Black Hawk helicopters, 184, 185–186
Black Liberation Organization, 93
Black Lives Matter, 39, 57, 96, 97–101, 104,
  108, 122
Black Lives Matter/Antifa riots, 39, 42, 60
Black-on-black crime, 111
Blair, Tony, 186
Border wall, 47, 65–67
Boudin, Chesa, 93, 94, 105
Boudin, Kathy, 93
Bowser, Muriel, 14
Breakthrough infections, 133
Brecht, Bertold, 61
Brinks truck, robbery of, Nanuet, New York
  (1981), 93
Brooks, Mo, 32
Budworth, Corey, 108
Burning of American flag, 40
Burrows, Matthew, 84
Bush, Cori, 24, 32, 33, 48, 108
Bush, George W., 4, 5
Bush lied, people died!, 5

California, 87–90, 106, 122
Cancel culture, 211
Capitol building "insurrection," 17–27,
  171–175
  Congressional Gold Medal award to
    Capitol police officers, 171
  deaths, 22–23
  Democratic response to January 6
    protest, 171–175
  exaggeration of scale of "insurrection,"
    24–27, 40
  Oath Keepers/Proud Boys, 18–20
  Ocasio-Cortez's claim she subject of near-
    death attack, 24
  Pelosi's scathing attack of Trump, 21
  prosecution of 49-year-old
    grandmother, 26–27

rejection of Trump's offer of 10,000 troops to guard Capitol, 19
setup by Democratic Party officials, 20
thefts of Pelosi's laptop computer and lectern, 18
we're the guys with the guns (refutation of Democrat's view of January 6 protest), 207
"white supremacist coup attempt," 24, 33
CARES Act. *See* Coronavirus Aid, Relief, and Economic Security (CARES) Act
Carlson, Tucker, 84, 85, 208, 210
Carson, Ben, 179
Carter, Jimmy, 5, 173
Carter-Baker Commission, 5, 161, 168
CBRE Group, 90
Centers for Disease Control and Prevention (CDC), 117
Chain migration, 78
Changing the demographics of voting population, 82, 84–90
Changing the world. *See* Reimagining the world
Charles Schwab, 90
Chauvin, Derek, 98, 99
Checks and balances, 2
Child tax credit, 148–149
China, 144
"China Virus," 116
Chinese virus research, 123–129
Ciattarelli, Jack, 199
Citizenship process, 61
Civil liberties, 134–138
Civil Rights Act of 1964, 54, 160
Climate change, 140–144
Clinton welfare reform, 149, 150
Clyburn, James, 202
Collins, Francis, 128
Communist-like re-education camps, 37
Contee, Robert, 113
Cooper, Anderson, 210
Corona control, 115–138
    breakthrough infections, 133
    CARES Act, 121
    censoring "misinformation," 120–121
    "China Virus," 116
    Chinese virus research, 123–129
    civil liberties, 134–138
    classic standoff (constitutional principles vs. transition to one-party state), 138

death rates per capita, 123
de facto martial law, 120
demonizing the unvaxxed, 129–134
face masks, 117–119
Families First Coronavirus Response Act, 121–122
flattening the curve, 119–120, 122
gain of function research, 125–127
"government by surrogate," 131
grant proposal "Understanding the Risk of Bat Coronavirus Emergence," 126
lab leak theory, 123–129
lockdown orders/mask mandates not necessary, 123
Operation Warp Speed, 116
Paul/Fauci verbal sparring, 125–126
Paycheck Protection Program and Health Care Enhancement Act, 122
Pfizer/Moderna vaccine, 116
political agendas, 143
reinfection rate, 133
relief bill, 121–122
reward-punishment-type system, 135
state control, 134–138
vaccination, 116, 129–134
vaccine passports, 134–135
See also COVID-19 pandemic
Coronavirus Aid, Relief, and Economic Security (CARES) Act, 121
Corporate taxes, 151
Countering Extremism Working Group, 179
COVID-19 pandemic, 10, 59, 82, 83, 105
    See also Corona control
Crime and punishment. *See* Reimagining the law
Crime epidemic, 113
Criminalizing parents, 196–197
Critical race theory, 95, 101–103, 194, 198
Cruz, Ted, 32
Cuba, 33, 86
Cuban refugees, 87
Culture, 62

DACA. *See* Deferred Action for Childhood Arrivals (DACA)
D'Angelo, Robin, 194
DAPA. *See* Deferred Action for Parents of Americans and Lawful Permanent Residents (DAPA)

Daszak, Peter, 123–124, 126, 128
Davis, Chris, 108
Davison, Ann, 199
Dean, Howard, 4
"Dear Colleague" letter, 31
de Blasio, Bill, 108–109, 134–135
Decriminalizing crime, 105
Deferred Action for Childhood Arrivals
    (DACA), 64
Deferred Action for Parents of Americans
    and Lawful Permanent Residents
    (DAPA), 65
Defunding the police, 107–109
Delusional threats, 211
Democratic Party
    accusing Trump of treason, 13, 14, 24
    allegation that Trump colluded with
        Russia to rig the vote,
        177–178
    American citizenship, 62
    assault on spirit of compromise that
        binds union together, 3
    attacking the voting system, 202–203
    attempt to establish tyranny of the
        majority, 176–177
    attempt to overthrow Trump
        presidency, 177–178
    authoritarian practices, 202
    blocking Trump from every holding
        public office again, 34, 35
    border wall, 65
    breach of civil rights in response to
        coronavirus, 134
    Bush lied, people died!, 5
    changing election rules in Pennsylvania,
        7–9
    changing the demographics of voting
        population, 82, 84–90
    character assassination of Trump, 75
    creation of one-party socialist state,
        211
    demonization of Trump, 34–37, 45,
        176
    deployed coronavirus as weapon
        against Trump, 115, 116
    disinformation and misinformation,
        36–37
    dismantling system of checks and
        balances, 211
    domestic terrorists and double
        standards, 40–43
    endorsement of Black Lives Matter, 97
    exaggeration of scale of "insurrection,"
        24–27
    Floyd, George, 98
    hyper-ventilating hatred of Trump, 7
    identity politics based on race, 62
    no-bail laws, 104
    outlawing "misinformation," 36–37
    Palestinian terrorists, 48–49
    ram-it-through approach, 159
    regarding rioters as "social justice
        warriors," 30
    reimagining the law, 105
    reshaping the electoral map, 160
    slander campaign against Trump, 9
    support for leftist riots, 30
    totalitarian vision and mentality, 136
    Tuberville amendment, 111
    2022 mid-term elections, 176–177
    violent crime in California, 89
    war in Iraq, 4–5
    zealous advocacy of socialist economics
        and political fascism, 212
Democrat's one vote majority,
    160–161
Department of Homeland Security (DHS),
    69
DeSantis, Ron, 136, 137, 176
Detention facilities, 74, 80–81
Digital Realty Trust, 90
Doctors Without Borders, 76
Dohrn, Bernadine, 93–94
Domestic terrorists, 40–43, 196
Douglass, Frederick, 52
Drug trafficking, 78–80
Duncan, Arne, 130, 131
Dyson, Michael Eric, 201

EcoHealth Alliance, 124
Economic policy. See Reimagining the
    world
Education. See Schooling
Elbright, Richard, 127
Elder, Larry, 101
Election Integrity Act of 2021, 164
Elias, Marc, 163
Ellison, Keith, 98–99
Emanuel, Rahm, 135
"Enhancing Public Safety in the Interior of
    the United States," 68
The Equality Act, 156–160
Equity, 56–60, 150
Existential threats, 211

Face masks, 117–119
Fall of Afghanistan
    arsenal of weapons stockpiled at
        Bagram, 184
    Bagram Air Base, 183–184
    Biden escalating public confidence that
        country would not fall, 183
    Biden partnering with Taliban, 186
    Biden's imbecilic decisions, 186
    date of withdrawal, 182
    domestic threat from alleged subversive
        opponents, 188–190
    ISIS suicide bombers, 186
    military stand-down, 188
    night vision goggles/Black Hawk
        helicopters, 185–186
    Pelosi's attitude toward Biden's actions,
        187
    spectacle of American incompetence
        and inhumanity, 187
    Taliban capture of Kabul, 183
    withdrawal of American air cover and
        intelligence, 182, 183
Falsification of America's history,
    49–54
Families First Coronavirus Response Act,
    121–122
Family Research Council, 179
Family reunification, 78
Fang, Christine, 29
Fauci, Anthony, 117, 124, 127
Fentanyl/fentanyl overdoses, 79–80
Fifteenth Amendment, 53
First Foundation Bank, 90
Flattening the curve, 119–120, 122
Florida, 123
Floyd, George, 39, 95, 98–99
Food and Drug Administration (FDA),
    116
For the People Act, 167–168, 176
Founding fathers, 1–2, 153
Freeland, Joel, 79

Gain of function research, 125–127
GAO. See Government Accountability
    Office (GAO)
Garland, Merrick, 38, 40–42, 196, 197
Garrison, Bishop, 179
Gemma, Peter, 69
Gender dysphoria, 159
Gender fluidity, 193
George Floyd case, 98, 99

Georgia
    COVID-19 casualties, 123
    Election Integrity Act of 2021, 164
    Georgia Special Committee on Election
        Integrity, 164
    MLB All-Star game, 167
    November 2020 elections and January
        2021 Senate runoff elections,
        161–164
    voting reform, 164–167
Georgia Special Committee on Election
    Integrity, 164
Ghani, Ashraf, 183
Gilbert, David, 93
González, Lorena, 199
Gordon, Terence, 107
Government Accountability Office (GAO),
    70
"Government by surrogate," 131
Gray, Freddie, 100
Green New Deal, 141–144
Guardian, 139
Guns, 112
Gwin, Mike, 12

Hanna-Jones, Nikole, 37, 52
Harlow, Poppy, 210
Harrell, Bruce, 199
Harris, Kamala, 37, 39, 79–80, 98, 104, 116
Hawley, Josh, 32, 41, 196
Hawley-Garland exchange, 41, 42
Hewlett Packard Enterprise, 90
Hirsi Ali, Ayaan, 179
Hitler, Adolf, 207
Holder, Eric, 169, 170
Homelessness, 151–152
Hoyer, Steny H., 13
Human infrastructure bill, 148, 200

I Alone Can Fix It, 206
Idaho, 123
Identity politics based on race, 62
Ignatiev, Noel, 194
Illegal aliens, 63
Illegal aliens. See Open borders
Immigration. See Open borders
Impeachment of Trump, 27–30, 34
Implicit bias, 56
India, 144
Inflation, 146
Infrastructure bill, 147–148, 151, 187
Ingraham, Laura, 137

Insurrection Act, 172, 180
Integration, 63
Irresistible Revolution (Lohmeier), 180
ISIS suicide bombers, 186
Islamophobic, 190

January 6 protest. *See* Capitol building "insurrection"
Japan, 62
Jayapal, Pramila, 33, 48
"Jim Crow 2," 167
"Jim Crow on steroids," 165
Johnson, Micah Xavier, 96, 97

Kaine, Tim, 35
Kao, Emilie, 158
Kavanaugh, Brett, 42
Kemp, Brian, 165
Keystone Pipeline, 142
Key to NYC Pass, 135
Khan-Cullors, Patrisse, 97
Kirby, John, 189
Kohistani, Mir Asadullah, 184

Lab leak theory, 123–129
Lafayette Square, 180
Lee, Barbara, 33
Lee, Sheila Jackson, 33
Leftwing teacher unions, 192, 196
Legal matters. *See* Reimagining the law
Lemon, Don, 132
Levin, Mark, 8
LGBTQI left, 156
Libertarian CATO Institute, 69
Little Sisters of the Poor, 159
Living wage, 142
Loeffler, Kelly, 161
Lohmeier, Matthew, 180
Looting, 104–106
Loudon County School Board, 195, 198
Lujan, John, 199
Lying, 147

MacDonald, Heather, 110
Maddow, Rachel, 168, 169
Madison, James, 153
Mail-in ballots, 5, 6, 16, 166, 168
Mann, Eric, 96
Markey, Edwin, 141
Marxism, 101, 150–152
Marxist organization of Sixties, 103
Massachusetts, 123

May 19th Communist Organization, 93
Mayorkas, Alejandro, 86, 87
McAllen, Texas, 81
McAuliffe, Terry, 198
McCarthy, Kevin, 175
McConnell, Mitch, 13
McGovern, Jim, 33
Mein Kampf (Hitler), 32
Merkley, Jeff, 42
Mexican cartels, 78–79
Mexico, 62
Mid-term elections (2022), 176–177
Milbank, Dana, 13
Military stand-down, 178, 188
Miller, Stephen, 71, 85, 172
Milley, Mark, 25, 172, 173, 180–181, 189, 190, 206–210
Minneapolis, Minnesota, 107
Minnesota Freedom Fund, 39, 97–98, 104–105
Misinformation, 36–37, 120–121
Mitchell, Chris, 84
MLB All-Star game, 167
Moderna vaccine, 116
Monahan, Terence, 106
Monopoly on the truth, 137
Morning Joe, 108
Mueller investigation, 178
Murphy, Phil, 199

National Action Network, 95
National Institutes of Health, 125
National School Board Association, 196
New England Journal of Medicine, 118
Newsom, Gavin, 131
Newsweek magazine, 140
New York City, 108–109
New Yorker, 209
New York Post, 104
New York State, 123
New York Times, 92, 93, 209
NIAID, 124
Night vision goggles/Black Haw helicopters, 185–186
1984 (Orwell), 206
Nixon, Richard, 88
No-bail laws, 104
"No cash bail" ordinances, 106
No Glory for Hate Act, 35
"No justice, No peace!," 42, 60
"No Justice, No Peace, No Racist Police!," 100

"Noncitizen movement" initiative, 84
Nord Stream gas pipeline, 143
November 2020 election, 197–199
"No Wisdom, No Courage!," 12
Nuclear power plants, 142
Nunes, Devin, 178
NY Post, 148

Oath Keepers, 18–20
Obama, Barack
    billion-dollar equity program to benefit
        farmers, 59
    border wall, 67
    born and bred radical, 64
    commitment to new anti-white racism,
        96
    critical race theory, 94–95
    DACA, 64
    DAPA, 65
    early life, 91
    red states/blue states, 91
    sworn to uphold the laws on the books,
        63–64
    white racism part of America's DNA,
        97
Obamacare, 144
"Off the Pigs!," 103
Omar, Ilhan, 48
"On Advancing Racial Equity," 56
Open borders, 61–90
    anti-Trump hatred, 82
    apprehensions of illegal aliens, 66–67,
        72
    barring media for accessing disease-
        ridden process centers, 81
    border wall, 65–67
    California, 87–90
    cancellation of order that DHS
        provide periodic reports on crimes
        committed by illegal aliens, 69
    cancellation of Trump's border-security
        measures, 69
    cancelling Trump's priority of
        deporting illegal aliens, 68
    chain migration, 78
    children, 73–79
    coronavirus cases among migrant
        children, 77
    COVID-19 pandemic, 82, 83
    Cuban refugees, 87
    DACA, 64
    DAPA, 65

Democrat's changing the
        demographics of voting population,
        82, 84–90
    deportation for criminals who
        committed aggravated felonies,
        68–69
    detention facilities, 74, 80–81
    drug trafficking, 78–80
    family reunification, 78
    fentanyl/fentanyl overdoses, 79–80
    Harris, Kamala, 79–80
    illegal immigrants being
        disproportionally represented in
        correctional system, 69–70
    McAllen, Texas, 81
    Mexican cartels, 78–79
    "noncitizen movement" initiative, 84
    obliteration of America's borders, 71
    policy of open borders frowned upon
        by other countries of consequence,
        90
    "Remain in Mexico" program, 68
    reversal of 62 Trump orders, 68
    secret transport operation, 84
    unaccompanied minors, 72, 76, 77,
        79
    U.S. Citizenship Act of 2021, 70
    zero-tolerance policy, 73–75, 77, 82
Open the Books, 184
Operation Warp Speed, 116
Oracle, 90
Orwell, George, 151, 206
Orwellian acts, 155–170
    abortion, 159
    Democrat's one vote majority,
        160–161
    The Equality Act, 156–160
    Georgia. *See* Georgia
    For the People Act, 167–168
    political correctness, 155
    religion, 159
    transgenderism, 158–160
Ocasio-Cortez, Alexandria, 24, 32, 35–37,
        48, 141
Ossoff, Jon, 161

Packnett, Brittany, 100
Palestinian terrorists, 48–49
Paris Climate Accord, 144
Partisan factions, 1
Paul, Rand, 124–128, 131
Paul/Fauci verbal sparring, 125–126

Paycheck Protection Program and Health
        Care Enhancement Act, 122
Pelosi, Nancy
        calling Trump's action regarding
            Capitol assault "seditious act," 21
        censoring "misinformation," 120
        "Dear Colleague" letter, 31
        demonizing the unvaxxed, 131
        "domestic terrorists," 173
        downplaying seriousness of COVID-19
            pandemic, 115
        embodiment of ambition to establish
            tyranny of the majority, 175
        The Equality Act, 156–160
        exaggeration of scale of "insurrection,"
            24
        Infrastructure bill, 187
        Islamophobic—one of "root causes" of
            January 6 protest, 190
        ordering troops to guard Capitol for
            more than four months, 25
        For the People Act, 167–168
        rejecting Trump's offer to provide
            10,000 National Guard troops to
            protect Capitol, 14
        response to January 6 protest, 173
        search for "domestic terrorists" in ranks
            of Capitol Police, 26
        "stormtroopers," 39
Pence, Mike, 13
Perdue, David, 161
Pfizer vaccine, 116
Planetary death, 144
Planned austerity, 140, 141
Police budget and personnel cuts, 108
Political correctness, 155
Politized military command, 180
Portland, Oregon, 108
Presidential election of 2020. See 2020
        presidential election
"Presidential Proclamation on the
        Termination of Emergency with
        Respect to the Southern Border of
        the United States and Redirection
        of Funds Diverted to Border Wall
        Construction," 66
Presley, Ayanna, 48
Progressives and reactionaries, 150–153
Proud Boys, 18
Psaki, Jen, 37
Puerto Rican terrorists (1954 shooting at
        House of Representatives), 173

QAnon shaman, 208
"Quality of life" crimes, 105
QuestionPro, 90

Radicals, 64, 147, 156, 191–192
Raffensperger, Brad, 162, 163
Ram-it-through approach, 159
Raskin, Jamie, 30–33
Reagan, Ronald, 88
Reason. com, 112
Rector, Robert, 149
Redistribution of wealth, 56, 57
Reimagining the law
        Black Lives Matter (BLM), 96, 97–101,
            104, 108
        black-on-black crime, 111
        Boudin's pro-criminal attitudes, 93
        crime epidemic, 113
        critical race theory, 95, 101–103
        decriminalizing crime, 105
        defunding the police, 107–109
        Democratic Party failures, 106
        George Floyd case, 98, 99
        guns, 112
        increased level of crime in inner cities,
            109–111
        looting, 104–106
        Minnesota Freedom Fund, 97–98,
            104–105
        "no cash bail" ordinances, 106
        police budget and personnel cuts, 108
        public outrage, 111, 112
        "quality of life" crimes, 105
        releasing criminals from prison, 105,
            106
        "reparations for slavery," 105, 106
        robbery of Brinks truck in Nanuet, New
            York (1981), 93
        "stand down" orders, 104
        Tuberville amendment, 111
        virulent haters of white people, 92
        Weather Underground, 92–93, 102, 103
        white Americans replacing blacks as
            targets of mindless bigotry, 92
        Whiteness Studies, 92
        white supremacy/white skin privilege, 92
Reimagining the world, 139–153
        American Families Plan, 145
        American Rescue Plan, 145, 146
        apocalyptic alternative (i.e. planetary
            death), 144
        child tax credit, 148–149

climate change, 140–144
Clinton welfare reform, 149, 150
Green New Deal, 141–144
homelessness, 151–152
inflation, 146
infrastructure bill, 147–148, 151
living wage, 142
Marxism, 150–152
most destructive spending spree ever, 144–150
nuclear power plants, 142
planned austerity, 140, 141
progressives and reactionaries, 150–153
raising corporate taxes, 151
single-payer health care system, 142
socialist wish-list, 148
universal basic income (UBI), 142
utopian schemes, 149
vagrancy laws, 152
whole system change, 140, 141, 143, 144
Releasing criminals from prison, 105, 106
Religion, 159
"Remain in Mexico" program, 68
"Reparations for slavery," 105, 106
Republican Party, 177
Reshaping the electoral map, 160
Reward-punishment-type system, 135
Rhodes, Stewart, 19, 20, 28
Ringing Capitol with 25,000 troops to face imaginary threat, 209
Riots, 39, 42, 60, 100, 104
Robbery of Brinks truck in Nanuet, New York (1981), 93
Robinson, Eugene, 37–38
Rouhani, Hassan, 206
Russiagate hoax, 163

Sánchez, Linda, 35
Sanders, Bernie, 46, 74, 145, 187
Sarsour, Linda, 42
Schiff, Adam, 25
Schooling, 192–197
    criminalizing parents, 196–197
    "domestic terrorists," 196
    gender fluidity, 193
    indoctrinating children in anti-American race theories and gender extremism, 193–195
    leftwing teacher unions, 192, 196
    parents' reaction to school system's "progressive" agendas, 193–195
Schumer, Chuck, 24, 34

Sears, Winsome, 200
Secret transport operation, 84
1776 Commission, 49, 52, 54, 178
Shakur, Assata, 97
Shamlin, Janet, 79
Sharpton, Al, 95
Sicknick, Brian, 22–23
SignEasy, 90
Single-payer health care system, 142
1619 Project, 49–50, 52, 178
Sixties radicals, 103
60 Minutes, 99, 117
Slavery, 50–53
Socialism, 151, 152
Socialist wish-list, 148
"Social justice warriors," 30
Soleimani, Qassem, 40, 205
Soros, George, 94, 105, 141
Southern Poverty Law Center (SPLC), 179–180
SPLC. See Southern Poverty Law Center (SPLC)
"Stand down" orders, 104
Stealth, 147
Steyer, Tom, 140
"Stop the Steal" rally, 14–16
"Stormtroopers," 39
Structural racism, 56
Students for a Democratic Society, 92
Sutton, Darien, 79
Swalwell, Eric, 28–30
Sweeney, Steve, 199
Systemic racism, 54–56, 62, 103, 105

Taliban, 181
    See also Fall of Afghanistan
Tarrio, Enrique, 20
Tesla, 90
Texas, 123
The Atlantic, 92
"The Big Lie," 32
The Hill, 76
The Intercept, 126
Third-party ballot harvesting, 16
Thomas-Kennedy, Nicole, 199
Times' 1619 Project, 49–50, 52, 178
Tlaib, Rashida, 48
Totalitarianism 101, 36
Transgenderism, 158–160
Treason, 13, 14, 24
"Treason to Whiteness is Loyalty to Humanity," 92

Trump, Donald
  Abraham Accords, 48
  appearing in public not wearing a
    mask, 118
  border wall, 65
  formation of 1776 Commission, 49
  impeachment, 27–30, 34
  killing of Soleimani, 205
  mail-in voting, 6–7
  "No Wisdom, No Courage!," 12
  Operation Warp Speed, 82, 116
  putting "America First," 35, 40
  six "Trump Place" residential buildings
    dropping his name, 35
  "Stop the Steal" rally, 14–16
  themes of presidency being patriotic,
    34–35, 40
  Twitter deplatforming Trump, 37
  ventilators, 115
  zero-tolerance policy, 73, 77
  See also 2020 presidential election
Tuberville, Tommy, 111
Tuberville amendment, 111
2020 presidential election
  Biden presenting himself as savior from
    dark cloud engulfing U.S., 45
  Biden's margin of victory, 11
  "the Big Lie," 32
  Trump lawsuit filed in Texas, 12
  Trump winning 26% of non-white
    vote, 38
  Twitter deplatforming Trump, 37
  two Biden campaigns, 46
2022 mid-term elections, 176–177
Twitter deplatforming of Trump, 37
Tyranny of the majority, 1, 153, 175, 177

UBI. See Universal basic income (UBI)
Unaccompanied minors, 72, 76, 77, 79
Unconscious bias, 56
"Understanding the Risk of Bat
    Coronavirus Emergence," 126
Undocumented immigrants, 63
United States of America. See America
Universal basic income (UBI), 142

Unsecured drop boxes, 16
Unvaxxed, 129–134
U.S. Citizenship Act of 2021, 70
Utopian schemes, 149

Vaccine passports, 134–135
Vagrancy laws, 152
Virginia's gubernatorial election, 197–198
Voluntary associations, 2
Voting reform, 167
Voting Rights Act, 169

Walker, Rich, Sr., 107
Wall on U.S.-Mexican border, 47, 65–67
Wall Street Journal, 124
Warnock, Raphael, 161
Warren, Elizabeth, 37, 74, 165
Washington Post, 92, 124, 126, 206–209
Waters, Maxine, 33, 99
Weather Underground, 92–93, 102, 103
We're the guys with the guns, 207
White Fragility (D'Angelo), 194
Whiteness Studies, 92
White skin privilege, 92
"White supremacist coup attempt," 24, 33
"White supremacists," 62, 110, 165, 195,
    210
White supremacy, 92
Whitmer, Gretchen, 19
Whole system change, 140, 141, 143, 144
Withdrawal from Afghanistan. See Fall of
    Afghanistan
World Health Organization (WHO), 47,
    117
Wuhan Institute of Virology, 124

Youngkin, Glenn, 198

Zero-tolerance policy
  gun dealers, 111
  illegally breaching U.S. border, 73–75,
    77, 82
Ziegler, Scott, 195
Zimmerman, Malia, 69
ZP Better, 90